The
GIST OF THE CULTS

*Christianity Versus
False Religion*

by

THE REV. J. K. VAN BAALEN, B.D.

Author of
*The Chaos of Cults,
Our Christian Heritage,* Etc.

Revised and Enlarged

WM. B. EERDMANS PUBLISHING COMPANY
Grand Rapids   Michigan

THE GIST OF THE CULTS
by THE REV. J. K. VAN BAALEN
Copyright, 1944
Wm. B. Eerdmans Publishing Company
All Rights Reserved

Copyright renewed, 1972
Nora M. Van Baalen

The Bible text used in this pamphlet is that of the American Standard Version copyright, 1929, by the International Council of Religious Education, and used by permission.

Sixteenth printing, May 1977

ISBN 0-8028-1205-8

PRINTED IN THE UNITED STATES OF AMERICA

CONTENTS

I. What It Is All About 4

II. Jehovah's Witnesses 8

III. The New Spiritism 16

IV. Theosophy 24

V. Christian Science 32

VI. The Unity School of Christianity 40

VII. Mormonism 48

VIII. British-Israelism 56

IX. The Christian Religion 62

I

WHAT IT IS ALL ABOUT

OF OLD God had a chosen people, to whom He made known his way of salvation. That people was Israel.

Slowly and gradually Israel lost the right interpretation of God's revelation. Passages of Scripture referring to the promised Messiah were said to speak of king Josiah or the prophet Jeremiah. Officially it was repeated over and over that man can save himself. All he has to do is to keep the law, something not at all impossible.

Thus Israel became like the nations from which it had been separated, for it had lost its revealed religion.

God's Son came into the world ... to give his life a ransom for many, to quote his own words. No wonder the Jews wanted none of Him: a ransom is paid for those who cannot redeem themselves; and the Jews had been taught that they were able to liberate themselves.

When God called Saul of Tarsus to become the **chief exponent of Christianity,** he was ill-prepared to assume this task. A pharisee of pharisees, he gloried in the doctrine of salvation by good works. Supernaturally converted, Saul became Paul, the great apostle and advocate of salvation by divine grace. It had been the good pleasure of **God, who separated me, even from my mother's womb, and called me through his grace, to reveal his Son in me, that I might preach him among the Gentiles, Gal. 1:15.** From then on Paul preached, **By grace have ye been saved through faith; and that not of yourselves. it is the gift of God; not of works, that no man should glory, Eph. 2: 8, 9.** Thus Christianity became the one great religion teaching salvation by divine grace and by grace only.

Later, as rulers became Christians and the Christian religion became popular, entire nations joined the Christian ranks either voluntarily or by government prompting. Christianity took over large sections of paganism faster than it could assimilate them. It greatly influenced the thinking of such peoples, but it in turn was impregnated by them. Slowly but surely the old idea that man is saved by his own good efforts gained foothold within the church of Christ.

That is not surprising. For the doctrine of salvation from sin and evil by good works is not only pharisaic; it is also pagan. It is in fact, the teaching of every known religion save the one revealed by God himself.

Toward the end of the middle ages the church had become badly corrupted. The church of Rome had never taught that man may be saved by his own works apart from the merits of Christ. In theory it had ascribed the major part of human salvation to divine grace resulting from Christ's sacrifice. Nevertheless, man had to add to the works of Christ. God had willed it so that man should earn part of his righteousness himself, should suffer a portion of his punishment in his own person. Gradually, however, greater emphasis was laid on man's efforts than upon the work of Christ.

When God raised up Martin Luther, a poor monk without social background, he was as ill-fitted for the task of preaching the gospel as Saul of Tarsus had been. For he was steeped in the Roman-Catholic doctrine of salvation by works.

Sin weighed so heavily with Luther that he spent all his time doing works of penance that he might blot out his transgressions. "True it is," he wrote in later years, "that I was a pious monk. So strictly did I keep the vows of my Order that I may say if ever a monk has entered heaven through monkery, then I also might have entered that way. All my fellow-monks who knew me will confirm that statement. If I had continued much longer, I would have tortured myself to death with vigils, prayers, reading and other work . . . . . Hence I now teach that such fool-works can never justify any one in the sight of God."

Whence that great change in Luther?

The change came about when the monk turned from the precepts of the apostate church to the writings of the apostle. When Luther understood Paul's words, **The just shall live by faith,** and discovered that those words, the theme of the epistle to the Romans, were a quotation from the Old Testament prophet Habakkuk, he underwent a change similar to that of the great apostle.

Upon the foundation of the re-discovered truth that man is saved by grace, which grace, a gift of God, is humbly received by faith, Luther rebuilt Christendom, and, with the aid of other Reformers, such as Zwingli and Calvin, made the Christian faith once more a potent factor.

But Protestantism lost out when it yielded to worldly modes of thought and living. And what has it come to in our own day? A multitude has arisen which outdoes the Church of Rome and the Pharisees of Jesus' day in teaching bold, unaided self-salvation. And they do it, partly by returning to the old pagan religions of the heathen world, and partly by robbing the gospel of its essentials though they still mention Jesus Christ and give him as much credit as fits into their manmade systems.

Thus the old struggle is still upon us.

It is the age-old contest between a supernaturally revealed religion holding forth a God-made salvation, and a deliverance that is man-made though it may occasionally point to Christ. It is paganism in a new form versus religion in its final, that is, its Christian form.

In the following pages some of the more popular substitutes for Christianity will be discussed.

It will be seen in many cases that the teachings here described are much farther removed from the truth for which Paul and Luther fought, than the Church of Rome has ever drifted from these teachings.

These substitutes for religion, it will be observed, are all the more dangerous because they parade under a Christian name.

Let the Church **instruct** its youth in the fundamental **teachings** of Christianity, that the breakdown of American Protestantism, and its slow bleeding by the **isms** which **do teach** false **doctrines**, may be stemmed.

"The small sects," wrote Dr. Clark in the 1937 edition of **The Small Sects in America,** "are sixty years behind the great progressive denominations and some of them are still back in the catechism period." Be that as it may, the "great progressive denominations" might note the fact that the Lutheran, Reformed, and other **churches which have** confirmation and catechism classes, in which the minister (who ought to know more about religion than the average Sunday-School teacher!) **teaches religion** to the youth of the church have lost few members to the cults we shall discuss.

Despite much pessimism prevailing in some circles in regard to the spirituality of the churches, however, we may here gratefully refer to a decided improvement in many places. Witness the following conclusion arrived at by "a rural social scientist and national director of the town and country department of the Congregational Christian Churches" after careful study of a recent 100,000 minister-poll of "Great Churches in America": "The final lesson of the Christian Century series is that rural ministers must teach and preach the Word of God . . . No half-hearted Sunday School can relieve the rural pastor of his duty of teaching his youth the Christian gospel."[1])

1. *The Christian Century*, Sept. 20, 1950.

II

JEHOVAH'S WITNESSES

JEHOVAH'S witnesses since 1931.
Prior to that known as **International Bible Students**.
Also formerly known as **Millennial Dawnists**.
At all times **Russellites**.

Most persistent of all anti-Christian sects, they stand on street corners on Fridays and Saturdays, mutely exhibiting their two magazines **Watchtower**, Announcing Jehovah's Kingdom, and **Awake**! And they refuse to salute the U. S. flag.

It all began with the Brooklyn haberdasher Charles Taze Russell who in 1874 suddenly emerged as "Pastor Russell"; who filled newpapers with syndicated columns adorned with the picture of himself with long, flowing beard; who published seven wordy volumes **Studies in the Scriptures**; who printed cartoons of himself as "the modern Daniel in the lion's den" (the "pastor" standing undaunted in the midst of crawling, snarling clergymen accusing him. "We have not ordained you"); who advertised meetings with "no collections" (only the devil's servants preached for salaries); who got himself into habitual trouble with the courts; who died in November, 1916, leaving behind a sizable fortune and a prophetic mantle which was thrown over the shoulders of ex-judge J. R. Rutherford.

"The Judge" completed the vast organization until in 1942 "the witness of and concerning Jehovah's Theocratic Government was carried on in practically every country of the earth . . . . and the kingdom publications distributed were published in 88 languages;" he denounced "the clergy", one and all, as "dumb dogs"; he had his followers ring

—8—

doorbells armed with little phonographs with records of five-minute addresses in "the judge's kind, clear voice"; he stated in 1921 that "the king of the north" in Daniel 11: 40, 41 means Great Britain, and in 1941 that he means the Nazis; he addressed the 1941 Convention of Witnesses at St. Louis in "an arena scheduled to hold 75,000 plus adjoining buildings", and "immediately 450,000 printed copies of his address were passed for distribution"; and he died on January 8, 1942.

The presidency of **The Watch Tower Bible and Tract Society** passed on to Nathan H. Knorr, the present leader of the organization, who has broadcast his address on **Freedom in the New World** over numerous hookups, and has added to the endless stream of swiftly printed and swiftly forgotten Russellite publications a 384-page book **The New World** ("you cannot afford to overlook the information this valuable book furnishes for your guidance"); and who has added a leaflet **Kingdom News**, which you may find on your doorknob when returning from an evening's visit.

And what is it all about?

And whence the fanatic zeal of these people who say that they "do not owe the U. S. government one bit of loyalty," and will gladly donate their time five evenings a week peddling literature?

And how did this weird system appeal to the religious instincts of thousands?

Russellism is a system of thought calculated to appeal to the religious pride of the uneducated among the unconverted.

"Use your reason," exclaimed Rutherford, "that's what God has given it for."

"Let us examine the character of the writings claimed as inspired (The Bible), to see whether their teachings correspond with the character we have reasonably imputed to God," wrote Russell. Always first reason, then the Bible must agree and follow!

—9—

This bold rationalism resulted in a summary dismissal of the entire labor of the Church prior to Pastor Russell's magic debut. Modestly, the man declared that it would be more profitable to peruse his volumes Studies in the Scriptures without reading the Scriptures than to reverse the process. Was not he the faithful and wise steward of Luke 12: 42 whom his lord had set over his household to give them their portion of food in due season?

One of the most notorious doctrines that Jehovah's Witnesses teach is that hell consists merely of "everlasting destruction." For years the Witnessess have agitated against "the Roman-Catholic doctrine of hell." That God should punish sinners with suffering is, they assert, not reasonable, since God is a God of love. The Christian doctrine of hell, therefore, is Satan's lie." According to Witness doctrine, Non-existence is "eternal punishment." There is no suffering — contrary to Jesus' words in Mark 9:47, 48. There is no "smoke of their torment" as in Revelation 14:11.

During the millennium all who have not heard the gospel will be given a chance of at least one hundred years to make up their minds. When they see that during the millennium the righteous are rewarded, that the blind, deaf, dumb, crippled will "develop new arms, legs, eyes, be given power of speech, and gradually develop a sound body," it is to be expected that few of them will refuse a gospel bringing these perfect earth-conditions. By accepting "the gospel" during the millennium they will make amends for former disobedience to the will of God, and consequently they will not receive "everlasting punishment." They will never die. Moreover, those living at the beginning of the millennium will receive this opportunity without first dying, hence: "Millions now living will never die."

And what of those who will not obey the gospel during the millennium? They will receive "everlasting punishment," which, however, does not mean eternal torment, but complete annihilation or extermination.

This doctrine of extermination of the wicked Russell took over from Seventh Day Adventism, which however, was

—10—

keen enough to understand that you cannot punish a non-existing, annihilated being, and therefore put the punishment (suffering) before the ultimate annihilation of the wicked.

Also from Seventh Day Adventism (which began some forty years before "Pastor" Russell appeared upon the scene) Russell took over the error of the unconscious condition of the soul between death and resurrection. This, too, however, he perverted. According to the sect we are discussing, man does not have a soul (contrary to **Numbers 21:4 Eccl. 12:7, Matt. 26:38,** etc.) but is a soul or spirit, and this spirit ceases to exist at death. In this Russell was not always consistent, nor did he explain how a non-existent soul can be resurrected.

Where do the Witnesses get their idea that Christ will soon erect the millennium, thus establishing the theocratic reign upon earth, and how do they conceive of the latter?

Russell taught that Christ is **not** divine. Originally he was an angel, Michael by name. Upon becoming the man Jesus he ceased to be an angel and became just man, though sinless man.

By his death he removed the penalty of death which followed from Adam's sin. This is called the at-one-ment. This at-one-ment opened the way for man to return to Scripture by his own free will and following his own common sense.

It is here that the out-and-out autosoterism (self-salvation) of Jehovah's witnesses appears. Man saves himself, and that from nothing more serious than quietly going out of existence (everlasting punishment they call that), because Jesus has opened the way by removing Adam's sin.

When Christ died he ceased being a man. His body, said Russell, either was dissolved into gases, or probably was kept somewhere "as a memorial" by God. According to Rutherford the latter undoubtedly happened. Christ now lives as a spirit. This spiritual being was given divine honor because of his former godly life. Rutherford, moreover, taught that "brother Russell" because of his excellent life,

—11—

"does not sleep in death, but was instantly changed from the human to the Divine nature, and is now forever with the Lord."

Christ was then appointed by God king of the nations. Since then the fight has been on of Satan and his organization versus Christ and his people, the contest being over world dominion.

Jehovah's witnesses, of course, are on Christ's side. By their testimony and their refusal to aid "the devil's organization" they prepare the world for Christ's return to establish his invisible, spiritual reign on earth.

At present "the devil's organization" comprises "the international politicians, great financiers and the church." Both the Nazis, "the King of the north," and the democracies, "the king of the south" have been "overreached by Satan," "and the consequences are that now in these last days the demons stand in control of all worldly governments on earth, and no human government is operating without demon control and without religion" ("religion" is part of the devil's tools, and includes every form of worship except Russellism).

It stands to reason that "Jehovah's witnesses" cannot takes sides in the conflicts. Any modern war is the devil fighting the devil, whereas the Witnesses belong to Christ. Saluting the flag is condemned, not because of disloyalty to the nation (any flag, any nation), but because it is considered an act of an idolatrous nature.

When Christ's theocratic rule will have been universally acknowledged there will be Peter's "new heaven and new earth," not a physically new heaven and new earth, but the real "New Order," "a new invisible power of control, Messiah's kingdom, and a new earth, society organized along new lines, to take the place of the old."

Thus Russellism appeals by its would-be eschatological views, its promises of ideal living conditions for all in the near future. The last war, Armageddon, a war of all politico-religious powers against Jehovah's witnesses, will soon result in Christ's overthrow of all the anti-Russellite forces. Then will be true freedom from want, and true freedom from fear. For the world will be "proof against all aggression and things which strike suddenly and without warning, including fire accidents, automobile and other traffic accidents, earthquakes, storms on land and sea, crop failure due to lack of rainfall or too much of it, floods, disease, old age, and death," and the world will be "rid of religion and its priests and ministers," who "put the people in fear of torment after death, either in a hideous 'purgatory,' or in a fire-and-brimstone hell filled with sadistic red-devils who use their pitchforks to see that none escape from the superheated flames."

The antichristian cults are "the unpaid debts of the Church." Truly, Jehovah's witnesses would not have grown so mightily, not even in a distressed world with its hunger for true peace and happiness, had not the churches in many instances made common cause with corrupt politics, and had not the so-called Christian nations become the easy prey of the demon of greed. And because the churches in all too many cases have refrained from instructing their membership in the true tenets of Scripture, the witnesses succeed in mixing their just grievances with a generous dose of thoroughly antiscriptural teachings.

Let us trace only the most glaring ones.

Most fundamental of all scriptural teachings are the two doctrines that stand or fall together, that of the holy Trinity and of the true Deity of Christ. If God is one God existing in Three equally divine Persons, than Paul's statement concerning Christ Jesus in Philippians 2:5 is correct, namely, that He was in the form of God, and therefore counted not the being on an equality with God a thing to be grasped, but emptied himself, taking the form of a servant, being made in the likeness of men.

If, on the other hand, Jesus was wrong in saying, I and the Father are One, John 10:30. He that hath seen me hath seen the Father, John 14:9, then Jehovah's witnesses are probably right that He first was an angel, and later became a mere man, and still later a spirit raised to the dignity of God as was also "Pastor" Russell.

Russellites should study the Christian teachings of the age before they make themselves guilty of such blasphemous distortions of the doctrine of the Trinity as to write: "There are some clergymen, no doubt, who are really sincere in thinking that Jesus was his own father, and the Almighty is the son of Himself; and that each of these is a third person who is the same as the other two, and yet different from them."

Ask a Russellite whether he believes that Jesus is divine. Press him as to the meaning of his terms. He will say, "He certainly was not Jehovah God."

But when at the heading of **Kingdom News** the Witnesses print **Isaiah 9:6, 7,** they omit part of those verses.

Why do they?

Because the omitted phrase states concerning the **child**, the **son**, whom they correctly admit to be the man Jesus, that his name shall be called **Mighty God, Everlasting Father.**

If Russellites really desire to learn the truth, let them consider that in Isaiah 44:6 Jehovah speaks, **I am the first and I am the last; and besides me there is no God;** while in **Revel. 1:17** the risen Son of Man says, **I am the first and the last, and the living One.**

In Jeremiah 23:5,6 David's future son, who is to reign as king, is definitely designated as follows: **and this is his name whereby he shall be called: Jehovah our righteousness.**

In Malachi 3:1 Jehovah of hosts says, **Behold, I send my messenger, and he shall prepare the way before me.** In Matthew 11:7-10 Jesus says that these words were fulfilled in John, who prepared the way before Jesus, and of whom, therefore, Zacharias had foretold **Thou shalt go before the face of the Lord** (Lord is **Kurios** in Greek, and **Jehovah** in the Hebrew Old Testament is **Kurios** in the Greek O. T.). Compare also **Malachi 4:5, 6** with **Luke 1:17**, and with **Matthew 17:11, 12, and Mark 9: 12, 13.**

There are far more references in the N. T. to the true deity of Christ, such as **Romans 9:5, I John 5:20**, but the foregoing suffice to show that the Russellite denial that Jesus is Jehovah-God is rank heresy.

Is it any wonder that men who err on the fundamental point of Jesus' true nature ignore His own statements concerning His resurrection body? Christ never rose in the body, say the "Witnesses;" whereas the risen Christ Himself said, **See my hands and my feet, that it is I myself: handle me and see; for a spirit hath not flesh and bones, as ye behold me having. Luke 24:39.**

Having no human nature, but being an invisible spirit, say the Russellites, Christ returned invisibly to the earth in 1914. But the angels said that He will return visible and in his resurrection body **(This Jesus ... shall so come in like manner as ye beheld him going into heaven, Acts 1:11)**; and from Patmos St. John said, **Behold, He cometh with clouds, and every eye shall see him, Rev. 1:7.**

In its worst days the Roman Catholic Church has never dared deny these fundamental truths; and the Russellites, instead of being witnesses of Jehovah, are farther removed from Christianity than Rome ever was, in spite of their continuous repetition of such language as, "the Roman Hierarchy, those children of Satan;" "the greatest racket ever in operation, the Catholic Hierarchy;" "Satan the Devil and his demons use the religious priests and clergymen as their principal means in opposing the true Christians who now announce the establishment of God's kingdom." [1].

---

1. A more complete discussion of Russellism and its arbitrary chronology may be found in the fourth revised and enlarged edition of my book, *The Chaos of Cults,* Eerdmans, 1962.

III

THE NEW SPIRITISM

THE new spiritism is not new.
It is very old.

New is only its better tone, and its closer approach to Theosophy.

Older spiritists denounced Christianity in vigorous terms, and admitted the vileness of many communicating spirits; this later spiritism ignores the Christian teaching completely. It can therefore afford to write in an even tenor and to appear kindly and dignified.

Of the Bible an older spiritist writer said, "To assert that it is a Holy and Divine Book, that God inspired the writers to make known His Divine will, is a gross outrage on and misleading to the public."

Concerning the Atonement another wrote, "Your atonement is the very climax of a deranged imagination, and one that is of the most unrighteous and immoral tendency."

Even Sir Oliver Lodge and Sir A. Conan Doyle, whose spiritistic writings were so avidly read during the first World War, had some unkind things to say of the church and its "terribly depressing doctrines," "odious conception so blasphemous in its view of the creator."

And now, with thousands of sons and husbands again on the far-flung battlefields, large numbers of men and women who are without the hope of the Scriptures, turn once more to those who have asked the dead, and they are given the age-old answer that after death all will be right, and there is nothing but endless improvement and evolution.

Death itself need not be feared, for it is only a gentle passing into a life very similar to the one just left behind.

Many soldiers who die on the battlefield awake as out of sleep and inquire in a somewhat bewildered way what has happened to them and where they are: those who have gone before are "kept busy" assuring them that all is well and they are still in the same world from which they have arrived.

Of Stewart Edward White's **The Betty Book** (1937), **Across the Unknown** ('39), and **The Unobstructed Universe** ('40), the second volume is introduced as **A Formula for Living,** and of the third the publishers state, "In answer to the desperate need of a stricken world, this book offers a new pattern for individual and social living—based on recapture of faith, not in the **thereness** of immortality, but in its **hereness."**

In these more than 900 pages God is not mentioned; only in the concluding pages some references occur to the Bible as "full of stepladders" to spiritistic truth.

Yet of **The Betty Book** John Haynes Holmes, minister of the Community Church at New York, "can only state that I find an honest report of firsthand and unquestionably genuine experience, had by sincere and intelligent persons, moved by sober scientific interest, embodying a system of spiritual truth as sane as it is sublime. The important thing is to recognize the reality of what is here set down."

Thus modernism, which itself has discarded the authority of Scripture in matters of faith, welcomes books which indeed contain sane advice concerning control of temper, worry and other faults, but which lead one far afield from all that Christendom has ever held dear, whether in its eastern or its western branch.

When the devil comes in velvet slippers, is he less dangerous than he once was when he decreed through spiritists, "We abrogate the idea of a personal God"? Are the thousands who have read the sixteen printings of **The Unobstructed Universe** which have come off the presses between September, 1940, and October, 1941, on the right track? Has Mr. White himself when he passed into the beyond found what he expected to find? Or has he, together with the thousands who followed his guidance, met with a disastrous disillusion because they have bypassed God' own revelation?

These questions will not down; too much depends upon their answer.

Mr. White, born in Grand Rapids, Michigan, in 1873, has for years been known as the talented author of many books of adventure and travelogues. During the last twenty years of his life, we are told, he has merely added to his travels through Africa and Alaska an itinerary far into another land, a territory more unknown, yet close around us.

It began in 1919, when Mrs. White—the "Betty" in the three books—was summoned by "Invisibles" (spirits in the beyond) to take psychic matters seriously and to develop her natural gift for communication with the dead.

For many years Mr. White and others have taken down a vast mass of what was revealed to "Betty," and when in 1939 the wife died, the husband continued his wife's explorations, got in touch with her, and at the age of 67 completed the message for the guidance of seekers after truth and comfort.

Fundamental in the White trilogy is the thought that "there is only one universe." Both "heaven" and "hell" are right here, hell being only suffering from frustrated urge, "since in the hereafter all are bound to desire the progress of evolution."

Betty states, "I am right here. There is only one universe. There is no other 'heaven'. It is only that you cannot see me. Your eyes are not attuned to the color, your ears to the sound. I am in the unobstructed phase of the one and only universe. That is all. It is only that my I-Am is separated from the obstruction that was my body. My world is your world **plus**."

Man is "a bit of individualized consciousness," and "the only rock" is "recognition of the creator as greater than the thing created," "acceptance of the Oneness of Consciousness as a whole."

Thoroughly pantheistic is the new spiritism as was also the old.

When asked how she could formerly pray the Lord's Prayer while yet "always beyond the anthropomorphic idea," Betty replies from the beyond that she was wont to address her prayer "to consciousness." "Did you think of consciousness with personality, warmth, such warmth as comes with personality, I mean?" "As though I were drowning in a great sea, and there was a shipful of people, any or all of whom could help me."

While in our earth-life, man has two bodies, the Alpha and the Beta body. The Beta is "the actual invisible substance which you have for long termed soul or spirit." It has weight and if you had scales you might weigh the medium before the cold goes into the room and after: the difference would be the weight of the cold which is the Beta going out in response to a magnetic call of another consciousness to your own. When this going out is done under proper conditions and in the right mood, great good may result, for one can get in touch with "the oversoul" only through the subconscious, which is in the Beta, while the conscious mind is in the Alpha body.

Spiritism, then, is the very opposite of Russellism with its rationalistic praise of "the intellect". White belittles the intellect, "the brain". It is "a marvelous mechanism," but effective only "in combination with the inner self". It is "a machine which must be worked by the other, wiser guiding consciousness."

Thus the man—the "person" is said to be in the Beta—is left a prey to all sorts of suggestions from the "spiritual world".

A fine, cultural soul like Mr. White does not receive vulgar, obscene, irreverent, silly information, as have countless other spiritists before him. And there are beautiful literary touches, fine illustrations in the White books. The mysteries of spiritistic phenomena become quite plausible events when he speaks on "Orthos and the Essences": Time, Space, Motion, Frequency, Conductivity.

Take a few samples.

Time has three aspects. The first is **sidereal time** (from Latin **sidera,** the stars). The term stands for our ordinary time, determined by the stars and ticked off by the clock. Already here, however, we know that there is a different aspect of time, which may be called **psychological time.** An hour is not always the same: five minutes may seem like sixty when we wait for a pot to boil. Fifteen minutes may seem endless when we nervously wait for a train to arrive; let the same fifteen minutes be spent in intent survey of beautiful surroundings, and the train arrives before we realize we have waited any time at all. Thus Time is elastic, not fixed at all.

There is also a third time, **orthic time** (orthos being the Greek word for right, correct, as most people know from the word orthodox (right in opinion). This orthic time, in which those live who have graduated from our life, is also "malleable"; it expands and contracts; it is a timeless present, of which we have a slight experience when we pace about oblivious to past and future moments. The "dead", therefore, are far from dead: they are like the Old Testament Jehovah who said "I Am", not I was or will be, but just **am.** Just plain being is the time condition of the hereafter.

There are also three aspects of **space.**

The first is determined by the **geometrical distance** between two points. **Psychologically,** however, that distance varies. Long if we walk it, footsore and weary; short if we ride over a concrete road in a modern car geared to do 70, 80, 100 miles an hour. When we sleep in a Pullman compartment we may awake at a distance of many geometrical miles, but all that space has vanished. What obstructs us is not the number of geometrical miles but "our inexpertness in telescoping them, or, if you will, telescoping through them".

In the third, or **orthic space,** those who have gone on before live in the same universe in which we dwell, but are minus the obstructions of the dense Alpha body, and they know that Space itself is not solid. They pass right through it at will.

There is also an **orthic motion.** In the universe in which we live, the obstructed universe, motion is real: the train may move faster and faster, though only up to a certain point. It may also stand still and yet be in motion, because it moves through space with the earth on which it stands. But in Betty's universe motion is obstructed neither by time nor space: "In orthos, motion is instant."

No wonder the wise spiritist does not fear death. He gladly anticipates it. It will be a permanent laying aside of all obstructions, something he has done quite frequently for a while, if, namely, he has developed the psychic aptitude of leaving the Alpha body and stepping out in the Beta. It is "a pleasurable releasing, quite different from the death-agony idea."

Besides, all the information from the other side points to the happy existence of the Invisibles. As the older spiritists spoke of seven spheres all around the earth as the layers of an onion around its core, so White speaks of different "levels" of existence hereafter. Those on the first level are guided on toward the next and more felicitous by those already inhabiting them.

Yes, it is all very attractive and quite scientific. It is as Darby concludes in **The Unobstructed Universe:** "so inclusive a philosophical structure, so closely knit, so airtight logically: one that proceeds through so wide a range of subjects and interlocks them all so perfectly that not a seam shows; and, with all that, expresses it so simply and so clearly." And there is such a gradual development from the first book through the second and the third, beginning with the demonstration that psychic phenomena are possible; continuing to show how it should be tried and what pitfalls to avoid; and working up toward a climax which leaves so little to be asked.

There are only one or two serious objections to the whole procedure.

The first objection is that all attempts at spiritism are strictly forbidden in the Scriptures, as any one may verify by consulting Levit. 19:31, Deut. 18:9-15; II Kings 21:2, 6; I Chron. 10:13; Isaiah 8:19-22; 19:3; Acts 16:16-18.

The passage in Isaiah condemns spiritism because it is asking the dead rather than seeking information from Jehovah; the passage in Deuteronomy states that it is seeking prophetic knowledge apart from the Christ Whom God was to reveal. Moreover, these passages state that God considered spiritism, the very ancient sin, of such a serious character that He destroyed seven nations for indulging in it; that Egypt, in punishment for its transgressions, was abandoned by God to spiritism; that it caused Saul's death as a divine retribution; that Israel was as much in danger of falling into this error as an apostate Christianity is today.

Only they who have been so thoroughly under the influence of modern unbelief as to reject the Scriptures as God's message to mankind, can fall into this sin.

The second objection follows from this first one.

If God forbade spiritism because it means obtaining information concerning the hereafter apart from Christ, we need not be surprised that the "formula for living" which it offers runs diametrically contrary to the divine formula for living and dying. And that formula of spiritism has been the same in all ages. It is unadulterated autosoterism. There is no need of repentance from sin in spiritism, and no need of a Saviour. The Mediator between God and man (I Tim. 2:5) is changed into a spiritistic medium. Evolution takes the place of salvation. The personal God, highly exalted above all creature and the Sovereign of His universe, is exchanged for the pantheistic notion of an impersonal cosmic consciousness. It makes a preacher's heart bleed with sorrow to see thousands turn for comfort to such naked paganism in a land dotted with Christian churches from Maine to California. Is it because the trumpet has given an uncertain sound that such things happen? Is this America's way of repenting when the divine judgments are so clearly upon us for our worship of demons, and the idols of gold, and of silver, and of brass, and of stone, and of wood **(Rev. 8:20)**?

It is therefore comparatively unimportant whence the information obtained by Mr. White and others derives. Suppose his undoubted verification of the source as being his departed wife and others with her was correct. In that case there still remains the fact that whatever information they imparted runs contrary to all that God has revealed in His word. As such his experience may be "scientific," but it cannot be "as sane as it is sublime."

However, this cannot be proven. The Scriptures are full of warnings against the evil influence of demons, fallen angels, the chief enemies of man. Paul states that our fight is against them even more than against flesh and blood **(Ephesians 6:11, 12)**. Other passages speaking of the ability of demons to influence men are **Genesis 3; I Kings 22:19-23; Ezekiel 28:11-19; John 8:44; I Corinthians 10:20.** The demons know about us and study our weaknesses. The Christian church in our day should recapture its conviction that the devil is **real**, not a fabulous notion of prehistoric days. It should revive a wholesome fear of this mighty enemy with his legions, and "put on the whole armor of God" against them.

And now we have not even referred to the host of fakers who parade under the semblance of spiritist "Reverends" and seers! We have considered spiritism at its best.

Better let spiritism severely alone, and turn to God for salvation through our blessed Lord Jesus Christ!

IV

THEOSOPHY

THEOSOPHY (divine wisdom) boasts of great things. It claims to be "nothing less than the bedrock upon which all phases of the world's thought and activity are founded (I. S. Cooper)." It is "a religion, a philosophy, a science, and yet, accurately speaking, none of these, for it is truly all of them and yet something beyond them (L. W. Rogers)."

In reality, theosophy is a form of spiritism.

As a mother first shapes her daughter's character, and in later years adopts some of her daughter's ways, so spiritism has given rise to modern theosophy and, of late years, taken over some of theosophy's distinctive points.

This should not surprise any one, since Blavatsky, the author of modern theosophy, began her career as a spiritist medium. For ten years she was under the control of a spirit calling himself John King. In 1857 "Madame" Blavatsky tried to found at Cairo a spiritistic society, but failed. Coming to New York in 1872, she sought co-operation with mediums; but just then so much fraud was exposed that she wearied of the spiritism of her day. In 1875 she founded the Theosophical Society in New York, aided by Colonel Olcott. She said of it, "It is the same spiritualism, but under another name." In 1882 Blavatsky and Olcott visited India together, and rounded out their system by adding Hindu and Buddhist elements. Blavatsky died in 1891, aged sixty years.

Her greatest successor was Mrs. Annie Besant, author, lecturer, traveler and scholar, who died in 1933 in her 86th year. Her outstanding claim was that her adopted son Krishnamurti was the new Christ or the re-incarnation of the World-Teacher.

For some years this good-looking Hindu, "young in body but not in spirit," enjoyed great popularity: women slept with his portrait under their pillows. He wrote a small book **At the Feet of the Master,** supposedly containing profound wisdom received directly from the Great Master. It is a booklet which has some good advice as to the balanced life, but throws man back entirely upon his own resources. In 1931, however, Krishnamurti, being an honest man, disclaimed his mother's assertion and refused to receive further adoration and gifts of estates. "I am not an actor; I refuse to wear the robes of a Messiah; so I am again free of all possessions. I have nothing but my creed." "To me," remonstrated the disappointed woman, "you will always be the Teacher;" but the rest of theosophists was free to look in another direction for the Promised One.

Let us, however, not run ahead of our story.

What does theosophy mean when it speaks of **Masters?** Why does it expect a new Messiah or Christ? Why does it parade as Esoteric Buddhism and at the same time as Esoteric Christianity? What is the **Karma** doctrine? What of **re-incarnation?**

Theosophy is out and out pantheistic. God is all, and All is God. Man is "a spark of divinity encased in matter." From the ancient orientals it learned to frown upon matter and to look at desire as the source of suffering.

Being pantheistic, theosophy knows no personal God. Buddhistically, it holds before man the great ideal of returning to the impersonal world-soul, losing all desire for earthly and human experience. The end reached, all evil will have been abolished.

This ideal will ultimately be attained by all human beings, but the process is long and laborious. When man dies he leaves behind a record of good and bad deeds. Action means **karma.** The law of karma, also called the law of causation, the law of cause and effect, of sowing and reaping, means that all action calls for other action. Evil desire calls for suffering, which alone is able to convince man of the wrongness of evil thought. And only good thought can destroy evil thought.

When man dies he dwells for a longer or shorter period of time in **devachan,** meaning, in heaven. Here he rests from his labors and is at ease. Sooner or later there awakes in him the desire to return to the earth that he may have further experience and work out his karma. So he is born once more as a babe, and in his new life he suffers for every wrong he has done in his previous life. Mrs. Besant, for example, taught that the untimely death of an infant was due the parents for unkindness to a child in an earlier incarnation. This doctrine is said to be in harmony with Scripture, for the disciples asked Jesus, **Rabbi, who has sinned, this man, or his parents, that he should be born blind**[1]?

Unfortunately, the number of incarnations "for the average monad" is said to be eight hundred. Theosophy is not niggardly with cycles of time! That some men are better than others is because their souls are older, more mature. They have lived many more times than the more elementary, cruder and younger souls. Potentially, however, every man is a Christ, and ultimately all shall be Christs.

In keeping with this theosophy teaches the enormous antiquity of the human race. The proper history of man began 18 million years ago. Theosophists publish maps of the world as it appeared 800,000 years ago, and again as it looked 11,500 years ago. The pyramids in Egypt are not 4000 years old as is ignorantly held by "O. P.'s" ("Ordinary Persons," being minus the occult information possessed by theosophists—the term is of A. P. Sinnett), but are the sole remnant of a civilization which disappeared 11,500 years ago as the result of a cataclysm when "the sea, which then covered what is now the Sahara desert, was driven eastward so as to completely deluge Egypt." Ten countries were torn

---

1. This reference to Scripture is erroneous 1. Because Jesus answered, *Neither did this man sin, nor his parents, John* 9:3; 2. because the disciples did not imply that the man might have sinned in a previous existence. They were steeped in the rabbinical teaching that a person may sin in his mother's womb, which the rabbis "proved" by a reference to Jacob, the "supplanter," who was born holding back his brother Esau by the heel.

asunder in the convulsion, and sank with their 64 million inhabitants.

When we inquire whence theosophy obtains all this "occult" knowledge, we are directed to the **Masters or Mahatmas**. In Tibet (until very recent times highly inaccessible!) lives **The Great White Lodge, The Occult Hierarchy, The Brotherhood of Teachers**. These Teachers, Masters, Mahatmas, Adepts, Initiates are "the finished products of human evolution," "divine men made perfect." They are "as far above ordinary mankind as man is above the insects of the field." These Brothers are ready to be absorbed into the impersonal world-soul, but, most kindly, linger on for the sake of "us, their younger brethren." In various ways they send out "floods of blessings over the whole world." No wonder Mrs. Besant asserted, "If there are no Masters, then the Theosophical Society is an absurdity."

But how do the Masters get in touch with theosophists?

Man, as we know him, has two bodies, **a natural body** and **a spiritual body**. The natural body is made up of four different and separable portions, and is subject to death. His spiritual body consists of three separable portions, each portion belonging to one of, and separating off, the three Persons in the Trinity of the human Spirit.

Let us limit ourselves to the "natural body."

It consists of **a physical body** with its **etheric double**, an **astral body**, and **a mental body**. These bodies occupy the same space as "the space in a bowl can be occupied by a sponge and by water that fills it, because the latter grade of matter interpenetrates the former." The physical body is the **body of activity**; the astral the **body of emotions,** the **desire-body;** the mental is the **body of thought.**

In sleep and in trance condition man leaves his physical body and, in his astral and mental bodies, dwells in the astral world. This astral plane is as "an envelope surrounding the earth" and at the same time penetrating it, "just as water penetrates the pores of a wet sponge. It is infused in all matter as a salt dissolved in water exists in association with all its molecules."

Observe here theosophy's spiritistic character as well as the theosophical nature of what we have called the new spiritism. The older spiritists taught that in trance condition the medium's subconscious mind gets into contact with the spirit-world through telepathy and clairvoyance. Theosophy and the newer spiritism hold that it is the man himself who leaves the physical body and visits the astral plane.

Having forsaken "spiritualism," Blavatsky taught that while man in his astral body visits the astral world, the etheric double (of the dual physical body) may be "abused" by a "disembodied entity living in the astral world, to re-establish his connection with the physical." This is mediumship, spiritism, which is dangerous; for the "disembodied entity" may or may not be a crude and undeveloped being.

Take the theosophist now. He does better. While in the astral body, he only gets in touch with pure astral beings. Man should reach the point where he can dwell with equal ease on the physical or on the astral plane. Above all, he should learn to remember his dreams, which are messages to him from more evolved beings.

Man's third body is the mental body. It requires a still higher stage of evolution to withdraw from both the physical and the astral bodies, and in the mental body to dwell in the corresponding mental world. This world is inhabited by devas, angels, the spirits, once human, who have graduated from the astral world.

The best work of the inspiring Mahatmas is done on the astral and mental planes. Each human life being like a day in school, and the normal interval between one life and another varying from a few score of years in the case of an undeveloped soul to twenty centuries or even more in the case of an advanced type, it stands to reason that the most advanced theosophists obtain the more occult instruction from the Masters. Finally, they are welcomed into the Great Brotherhood of Teachers.

Above all these Mahatmas there is **One Supreme Teacher.** When this **World-Teacher** deems the race ready to receive a new and higher revelation, he looks for a very advanced human being, ready for initiation, takes control of his body, and lives in and speaks through that body. This for the benefit of the race.

There have been three human races thus far: the **Lemurian**, the **Atlantean**, and the **Aryan**. Each one of these has developed several subraces. The present, or **Aryan rootrace,** has now its **fifth subrace, the Teutonic**. It is soon to be followed by a sixth subrace. The present subrace is the **intellectual man** (Jehovah's witnesses, rejoice!). However, the coming race will be that of the **spiritual man** (Witnesses, give heed!).

At the beginning of each subrace the Supreme Teacher of the World becomes incarnate in order to contribute to the evolution of that race. Since the present Brotherhood-feeling and Unity-efforts pervading the world indicate a new beginning, we may confidently anticipate an early incarnation of the Teacher. He has been present five times during the existence of the Aryan race: As Buddha (India, first subrace), as Hermes (Egypt, second subrace), as Zoroaster (Persia, third), Orpheus (Greece, fourth), and finally as Christ, when the Palestinian Jesus surrendered his body to the World Teacher upon the occasion of his baptism.

Since each race and subrace is more evolved than the former, we are soon to see a Messiah who will bring a greater message than any before him have announced. At the same time, however, it appears that since all Messiah's are indwelt by the same Supreme Teacher and weave the same fabric, that which is Esoteric (designed for those on the inside, the initiate) Buddhism is also Esoteric Christianity. "Whether the person pray to Buddha, to Vishnu, to Christ, to the Father, it matters not at all," decreed Annie Besant. "The Brotherhood of Religions" is the first plank in the theosophic platform. "Every religion has a note of its own, that it gives for the helping of the world ... blended together they give the whiteness of truth, blended together they give a mighty chord of perfection (Besant)."

Theosophy poses as a philosophy. Yet it is not difficult to disprove its philosophical tenets. It suffers from a mixture of fundamental principles which are as different as fire and water.

1. It is pantheistic and as such considers God a spiritual being. At the same time, however, it speaks of the material side in the impersonal Godhead, and this material is thought of as ethereal, neither altogether spiritual nor wholly material; and theosophy loses itself in the most intricate speculations on the "masculine" and the "feminine" in this impersonal deity.

2. It cannot account for the human intellect, will and personality, since man is a spark of the impersonal godhead. Pantheism and the polytheism of the Hindus are mixed in theosophy with feminine lack of logic.

3. The reincarnation theory is untenable. It is beyond comprehension that the human soul, after having escaped through evolution, first into the astral world, and then into the still higher spiritual world of **devachan**, should long for the lower life in the grossly material body. Why should man, who is on the way to escape from earthly sorrowful experience, "thirst for more experience, such as may only be gained on earth"?

4. The karma doctrine is untenable. Experience teaches that it is not correct to ascribe all suffering to evil done in a former period of existence. We suffer much as a result of the misdeeds of others.

5. There can be no merit in suffering for sins done in a former existence because the sufferer has no knowledge of his former life, cannot trace cause and effect. The assertion that the soul remembers although it cannot communicate through the brain, is a mere subterfuge.

6. The karma theory is unjust. Why should one suffer the penalty of evil desires by starving them in the astral world and later on suffer another penalty in lives to come? Here

the spiritism of Blavatsky's first and the Buddhism of her second period have been joined together in a fruitless effort to arrive at unity.

That keen thinker and brilliant lecturer, the late Dr. Francis L. Patton, president of Princeton University, later president of Princeton Theological Seminary, was asked by a lady after one of his lectures to give her the strongest argument against theosophy. "Madam," said Dr. Patton, "the strongest argument against theosophy is that there is no argument in its favor."[1]

And there is far more. However, this small booklet is written by an "O. P." for his fellow O. P's. It is written, not from the standpoint of philosophy, but as an avowed warning by a Christian pastor to those who are in danger of losing their hold on Scripture, or are so ignorant of the fundamental teachings of the Bible as to think that any system may do which talks mystically and quasi profoundly and quotes Scripture occasionally. Observe then:

1. That Christ has warned against false Christs who would come in His name, **Matthew 24:23-27.**

2. There can be no "new revelation" beyond that in Christ Jesus. See **John 1:14; and 14:9; II Cor. 4:3, 4; Col. 1:19-28; Heb. 1 and 2; I John 5:20; II John 10, 11; Jude 3; Rev. 22: 18, 19.**

3. There is no re-incarnation, either of Jesus or others, **Heb. 9:26, 27.**

4. There is no brotherhood of religions, **Gal. 1:8; II John 10, 11.**

5. And, thanks be to God, there is no deliverance through the law of karma, but by divine forgiveness, **Isaiah 1:18; I John 1:9.**

---

1. Machen, *What Is Christianity? Eerdmans*, 1951, page 70.

V

CHRISTIAN SCIENCE

AS RUSSELLISM is the most arrogant of the false systems posing as Christian, so "Christian Science" is the most stupid.

This statement is not an Error of Mortal Mind.

Neither does it attack the gentle reader as a flood of Malicious Animal Magnetism.

We expect to demonstrate its truthfulness shortly to the reader's satisfaction.

We do not claim, however, that there is no truth in Christian Science. The devil is far too cunning to come with unadulterated error. An element of truth is mixed with and neutralized by so much falsehood that it is rendered harmless from the standpoint of the father of lies.

Thus when a lady shakes a warning finger at the present writer and says, "O sir, I am afraid you do not understand Divine Science; we certainly can destroy evil with our thought," she is speaking a partial truth—in the second half of her statement. Suppose you are tempted to think unclean thoughts, you will surely be able to destroy the unclean thoughts, and you will surely be able to destroy the temptation, for the time being at least, by substituting wholesome thought and force your mind in a different direction. So also physical pain may at times be eliminated from one's consciousness by sheer will power.

But all that is something very different than Christian Science though its adherents exploit that well-known element of truth.

The error of Mrs. Eddy's brainchild is that it denies the reality of all evil. It asserts that no evil exists in "Science."

Then it turns completely around and speaks of evil as much as any other philosophy or religion ever did.

This has bewildered many students of Mother Eddy. The astonishment is due, as "Scientists" will affably affirm, with a look of profound wisdom, to lack of understanding on the part of the puzzled inquirer. He has not "demonstrated" the truth of Divine Science; hence cannot grasp its profundity. In other words, only confirmed Scientists can understand Christian Science.

The truth of the matter is that Christian Science is not a philosophy, but only "an elaborate idea." It has gone wild on its fundamental thought that "God is all. All is God." "God is All-in-all. God is good. God is Mind. God, Spirit, being all, nothing is matter. Life, God, omnipotent good, deny death, evil, sin, disease."

This is Eddyism in a nutshell. It has stressed its pantheism to such extremes that it denies the reality of all that is not God. Christian Science is "pantheism gone to seed." No ordinary pantheist—and his name is Legion—has ever gone the length of Mrs. Eddy, that of denying evil in its every form because "God is All-in-all."

In a rare moment of insight and humor Mrs. Eddy once quoted Bronson Alcott who said that her **Science and Health with Key to the Scriptures** "no one but a woman or a fool could have written." However, being a foolish woman was not her chief "Error." She made matters worse when she veered around and admitted that even Christian Scientists in their present stage of development suffer from "Mortal Mind." As Error of Mortal Mind (Mrs. Eddy Loved Capitals) she branded every form of apparent evil as well as all things material. Since only God has reality, and God is Spirit, Principle, it is the task of every Christian Scientist to "demonstrate against" every form of evil and matter, that is to say, to prove its fictitious character by driving it out by divine thought.

But Mrs. Eddy failed to explain one thing—and we challenge every "C. S. B." who goes up and down the land lecturing on "divine" science, to account for it:

If God is the only reality, and God is good, how can there be any mortal mind to think evil, even an unreal evil?

Christian Science, then, is so palpably false in its basic structure that it is indeed stupid. Some Oriental religions asserted that evil has always been, that it proceeds from an eternal evil god. That statement denies the real divinity of the opposing "good God," since neither god is supreme. Yet it is far more respectable than the assertion that evil cannot exist, only to pose evil in the same breath and to ascribe it to an evil mortal mind which cannot exist in an evilless, matterless, all-good-God universe.

With this simple criticism the entire profundity of this structure tumbles down like Jericho's walls.

Shall we then ignore Christian Science as an innocent plaything, a travesty on logic? Alas, it cannot be done. Eddyism has done too much damage. It allures the gullible American public by its high sounding name: what woman (75 per cent of its devotees are women) would not like to be a scientist and a Christian all rolled in one, and that at such little expenditure of effort? It is not even necessary today to pay $200 for a course of six lessons, as it was in the days when Mother Eddy taught in her "Metaphysical College" at Boston, that venerable seat of American intelligence. And who, desirous of a shortcut to the elimination of evil, would not gladly be lulled to sleep with the affirmation that all this talk about sin, about death and sickness and suffering, need not alarm any one, since it has no reality?

Our Bible tells us that Satan is **able to fashion himself into an angel of light. It is no great thing therefore if his ministers also fashion themselves as ministers of righteousness, II Cor. 11:14, 15.** What could be more pleasing to Satan than to hear his existence denied while those who do so subvert the word of God into its very opposite?

Consider the **Glossary** at the end of the book **Science and Health.** Common words occurring in Scripture as in everyday speech are there given a meaning which they never had. **Adam,** we are told, means **Error; a falsity; the belief in "or-**

iginal sin," sickness and death; evil; the opposite of good—of God and His creation; etc. Christ means the divine manifestation of God, which comes to the flesh to destroy incarnate error. Thus Paul's words, For as in Adam all die, so also in Christ shall all be made alive, I Cor. 15:22, are said to mean, As in error all die, so in Truth shall all be made alive. That is not a Key to the Scriptures except that it forever locks entrance to the plain sense of Scripture. When the Bible speaks of Elijah it does not mean "prophecy" but a prophet of flesh and blood; wine never did mean "inspiration; understanding, Error; fornication; temptation; passion" (quite a variety of meanings, at that!).

Christ, according to this system, never died; for death is "error," and Christ is a spiritual idea, whereas Jesus was a "corporeal thought" of Mary. Let alone the folly that there could have been no Mary if God is All and "uncorporeal spirit"; what we must think of this way of dealing with Scripture?

Burial becomes "corporeality and physical sense put out of sight and hearing; annihilation. Submergence in Spirit; immortality brought to light." Thus Jesus' death, burial, and resurrection all become fictitious notions of that Mortal Mind for which there is no room in this ultrapantheistic system, and which it nevertheless recognizes in spite of its most fundamental tenet. "His disciples believed Jesus to be dead while hidden in the sepulchre, whereas he was alive, demonstrating within the narrow tomb the power of Spirit to overrule mortal material sense," says **Science and Health.**

"The atonement," wrote Mrs. Eddy, "is a hard problem in theology, but its scientific explanation is that suffering is an error of sinful sense which Truth destroys."

Prayer becomes merely "desire." Naturally so: for there is no personal God, no God distinct from us. "Shall we ask the divine Principle of all goodness to do His own work? His work is done." "God is not influenced by man."

Prayer, then, is merely concentration. In this respect Christian Science agrees with pantheistic Theosophy, whose

Mrs. Besant wrote, "The action of prayer—which is concentrated thought." "The mere habit of pleading with the divine mind, as one pleads with a human being, perpetuates the belief in God as humanly circumscribed—an error which impedes spiritual growth," decreed Mrs. Eddy. While Mrs. Besant wrote of the advanced theosophist, "Then he learns that Divinity lies hidden within himself, and nothing that is fleeting can satisfy that God within; ... he has risen above all prayer, save that which is meditation and worship; he has nothing to ask for, in this world or in any other."

What importance, then, have the words of the Christian Science Board of directors when in June, 1943 they "placed prayer at the top of the list of defensive and offensive weapons that free-thinking peoples are counting upon to win the global war against oppression and suppression"? Will American Christians, who fall for "such a wonderfully reverend atmosphere, and so solemn" in a "church" of this type, never learn that when two people use the same phrases they may yet mean something entirely different and opposite?

And if one wonders why Mrs. Besant and Mrs. Eddy sound so much alike, is it difficult to understand that pantheism underneath is always much the same? Besides, Mrs. Eddy as well as Mrs. Blavatsky was in her earlier years a spiritistic medium. "Doctrines of demons" is what the Bible warns against, I Timothy 4:1.

One might well ask, however, how Mrs. Eddy could be so glaringly inconsistent as to write of the impersonal Principle called God while in the same sentence referring to "His own work"? The answer is that to Christian Scientists there is no inconsistency in this. It all runs smoothly if one will but bear in mind that Mrs. Eddy continually uses two sets of language, the language of Divine Science, and the language of mortal mind. To the first things are so different than they appear to the second. This is "the trick of two languages," which makes Eddyism seem profound to those who do not understand, dishonest to those who see through it.

In this way Christian Scientists can live a normal life, and show preference for church buildings in white marble or its substitute; they can eat and drink and wear fine clothing: for it is better while being "under the tyranny of Mortal Mind" to substitute a more refined error for a more gross one. As long as we **think** we have a hungry stomach it is more convenient to fill this imaginary empty stomach with unreal costly food than to suffer the additional suppositious error of being hungry. Ultimately, however, Scientists will "demonstrate against" every conceivable material **error. Then nothing but Divine Truth, Science, will be left.**

Is it any wonder that some of us laugh at the comfortable admission that at the present stage of imperfect understanding of "Science" only sickness can be demonstrated against, and not, for instance, luxuries?

A German poet once said that **Weltgeschicht ist Weltgericht**; that is to say, "The world's history is the world's judgment." While this is not always true within the narrow space of a few years, it certainly holds of Mrs. Eddy, founder of Christian Science.

Born in 1821, for many years a neurotic patient, twice unfortunate in marriage, Mrs. Eddy did not "arrive" until she was sixty-one years old, had been left by one husband, buried two, the last one killed by "arsenic mentally administered." She who had denied the reality of physical death had to admit that much.

Had she been satisfied to abide by the Christian faith she had been taught in her youth, Mrs. Eddy might have come to a quiet and dignified old age.

But she was proud and ambitious: "I founded a Church of my own," was her boast. She was greedy: She was forever re-arranging the contents of her book, and upon the printing of a new edition immediately pronounced all former editions worthless; in this way she realized a million dollars on her book; she sold souvenir spoons, and demanded that all "Christian Science practitioners" pay her $100 in advance and ten per cent annually on the income derived from practicing "healing;" and left an estate of three million dollars. She was envious of her position to the point of vindictiveness against those who had been her loyal handmaidens [1]).

Her old age was spent in loneliness and dreadful fear of "malicious animal magnetism." Animal magnetism she had defined as "the criminal misuse of human will power," "the voluntary or involuntary action of error in all its forms." She who had denied the reality of all forms of evil spent her declining years in fear of the magnetism directed against her by her chief supporters, and had faithful practitioners watch the night through, seated outside her door, to counteract the poison aimed at her by her supposed enemies. She lost all ease of mind, distrusted her surroundings, could get no comfort from the book she had sold at high cost for the consolation of others; and died a very old and sad, toothless woman of eighty-nine years.

Surely, there is divine nemesis in all this. **God is not mocked: for whatsoever a man soweth, that shall he also reap. Gal. 6:7.**

Had Mrs. Eddy remained satisfied to heal minor mental disturbances through the wise application of psychology, as did her teacher P. P. Quimby before her, and as is done today by every psychiatrist, she might have proved a blessing to mankind. Her name might well have been honored as a pioneer's name in the history of mental healing.

But she must needs exploit the truth of the power of mind over matter to the point of denying every human experience. When she found the Bible to run contrary to her pet theory, she did not hesitate to change the meaning of the English vocabulary in order to make the people's Bible fall in line with her ungodly teachings; she brushed aside all medical and surgical science as Error of Mortal Mind. The result has been a system which has advertised its testimonials of cures as does any ordinary patent medicine; which

---

1. Read the account of Mrs. Eddy's treatment of Mrs. Stetson in *Mrs. Eddy. The Biography of a Virgin Mind* by E. F. Dakin. Schribner's 1930.

has indeed helped many, but caused others to die of the diseases of which they had been healed (as other patent medicines and systems of faith healing) ; and which has caused the death of innocent children who might have benefited by timely medical assistance[2]; it has robbed its devotees of the only comfort that holds in death, the comfort that one belongs to his faithful Lord and Saviour Jesus Christ.

That comfort was singly lacking in Mrs. Eddy's own case because she had arrogated for herself divine honor, informing her followers that she was to be addressed as Mother, and the Lord's Prayer should be directed to **Our Father-Mother God.**

And what of the moral influence of this wicked system?

Since belief in matter is error, Mrs. Eddy taught that marriage must continue "until it is realized that God is the Father of all," but, even while it lasts, the ideal is a childless union.

Has not the Bible said something in warning against **doctrines of demons . . . forbidding to marry, I Tim. 4:3?**

---

[2]. A partial account of cases that have come before the U.S. Courts may be found in Stephen Paget, *The Faith and Works of Christian Science;* W. A. Purrington, *Chr. Scie., an Exposition of Mrs. Eddy's Wonderful Discovery, including the legal aspects, a Plea for Children and other Helpless Sick;* and other sources.

VI

THE UNITY SCHOOL OF CHRISTIANITY

THEY who are of the opinion that it makes no difference what one's philosophy is as long as one "lives right"—let them stop and consider.

Darwin's idea of "the survival of the fittest" was taken over by Nietzsche. German scholars interpreted Darwin's ideal as the ideal of the survival of the fittest race, where the British had interpreted it to mean survival of the fittest individual. Brutal, blustering Prussian militarists decreed that the German "race" was superior. Hitler presented Mussolini with a de luxe edition of the works of Nietzsche. The result of it all is with us today. The haughty Darwinian hypothesis of the evolution of humanity, which Haeckel called "Darwin's great Anti-Genesis," has rebounded upon the human race and caused its downfall.

Likewise, there is a common philosophy back of the similarity existing between "New Thought," "Christian Science" and "Unity."

We must go back a century and a half for the beginnings.

From 1774 to 1814 Franz Anton Mesmer, the great German physician, wrestled with the problem of psychotherapy, as we call it today. Incidentally he discovered the power of one man over another. But he failed to understand that power, and ascribed it to "magnetism," later on to a fluid supposed to emanate from the healer and to affect the patient.

Count Maxime de Puységur discovered in 1784 that Mesmer's alleged magnetic fluid is indeed a power of the human mind, and he opened up the large field of hypnotism and somnambulism.

Charles Poyen, a French hypnotist, introduced the revived mesmerism to the gullible public of the New England states, A. D., 1836.

Phineas Park Quimby heard Poyen lecture at Belfast, Maine. Poyen told "Park" that he had vast psychic powers. Quimby, the clockmaker, began to experiment with sick folk, used his rare hypnotic power upon suffering New England, and in his own right "discovered" the power of mind over matter.

Quimby became the pioneer mental healer of his day in the United States. It was not medicine, he asserted, but faith in medicine which healed people. It was the faith that was important. He wrote his philosophy in ten volumes of longhand, which he generously lent to his disciples and patients.

When Quimby was sixty years old and she forty-one, Mrs. Eddy came to Quimby.

To Quimby came also Julius Dresser.

Mrs. Eddy plagiarized the Quimby manuscript after the good man's death, and renounced him concerning whom she had formerly written poetry: "To P. P. Quimby Who Heals the Sick as Jesus Did;" "P. P. Quimby rolls away the stone from the sepulchre and health is the resurrection." Mrs. Eddy called her revised Quimbyism **Christian Science.**

Dresser named his **The New Thought.**

Myrtle Fillmore, states the Unity literature, "heard a lecture by a now all-but-forgotten metaphysical lecturer that marked the turning of the tide in Mrs. Fillmore's life, and through her, in that of others"—and decided to call her "discovery" of health and harmony through "practical Christianity" **Unity.** "Practical Christianity," by the way, was the name then in use in the West for New Thought. "Unity" was a novel name, apt to spread the old ideas in a rather virgin territory.

Thus these three movements have a common pantheistic **origin.**

No, Unity is not quite Christian Science. For one thing, it is not quite as foolish. Christian Science says that the visible world is an illusion of Mortal Mind; New Thought and Unity declare the visible world to be an expression of God's handiwork. Christian Science is pantheism denying the reality of the material world; Unity is pantheism asserting the divinity of the material world.

The Unity literature warns that "many of those not acquainted with the distinctions of metaphysical thought class Unity with Christian Science because of a common emphasis on healing; nevertheless Unity, in nearly all its expositions of Truth, is quite distinct from Christian Science. To class them together is a mistake."

Then, being always friendly and loving, Unity continues, "While the Fillmores were not students of Mary Baker Eddy, nor connected with the Christian Science church in any way, a friendly feeling is always expressed by Unity and its workers toward Christian Science and all other religions. 'God is no respector of persons' or of sects."

Thus Unity agrees with Spiritism, Theosophy, Bahaism, and kindred pantheistic cults in acclaiming all religions of equal value; with pantheistic Christian Science and New Thought it lays emphasis on healing through the mind. With pantheistic Theosophy it teaches the reincarnation of the soul in future lives. With theosophy it also believes in vegetarianism: why kill life, which is divine, to obtain food?

Charles Fillmore was a cripple from infancy. He suffered from a hip disease. Besides, he had curvature of the spine, and was deaf in his right ear. When his wife contracted tuberculosis, they lived for six years in Texas and Arizona, hoping to find health in the arid climate. During a boom Mr. Fillmore amassed a fortune of $150,000 in real estate, but during a depression he lost it all. The members of his family also fell ill: penniless and sick, they saw little ahead that was hope-inspiring. It was then that Myrtle heard the lecture already referred to.

From it one idea stood out in her mind: "I am a child of God, and therefore I do not inherit sickness." "This idea was far reaching," says the Unity pamphlet.

Indeed it was. Myrtle Fillmore's tuberculosis vanished, "and she began to heal her children and neighbors." "Gradually the influence of Mrs. Fillmore began to take on the aspects of a religious movement." The husband also became interested in his wife's work. He, too, regained his health. In 1889 they decided together not to take any more chances with real estate, but to make others share in their religio-medical find with its resultant: material prosperity.

Myrtle Fillmore "passed on" in October, 1931. Charles later married his secretary Cora Dedrick, "of invaluable help to him in his work." He continued writing, and also believing that he would not die, until he, too, deep in the nineties, joined the ranks of the immortals on July 5, 1948.

That Unity is closely related to Christian Science may be learned by comparing the following quotations.

Mrs. Eddy wrote: "Sin, disease and death have no foundation in Truth." DEATH—An illusion."

Charles Fillmore wrote: "God is not dead; he does not recognize or countenance death; neither does man when freed from its delusion . . . The first step in demonstrating over death is to get the belief entirely out of the mind that it is God-ordained, or that it is of force or effect anywhere in the realm of Pure Being. The next step is to live so harmoniously that the whole consciousness shall be not only resurrected from its belief in death, but also so vivified and energized with the idea of undying life that it cannot dissolve or separate."

Small wonder, then, that Charles W. Ferguson wrote of a home in which the husband, a rather distinguished professor of biology, holds Unity literature in contempt, while the wife worships it: "I know that the wife fully expects her rosy daughter to live to be five hundred years old and to die of her own accord if she dies at all."

Again, Mrs. Eddy wrote: "What is God? God is incorporeal, divine, supreme, infinite Mind, Spirit, Soul, Principle."

Mr. Fillmore's words are: "The truth is, then: that God is Principle, Law, Being, Mind, Spirit, All-Good." And: "God is individually formed in consciousness in each of us, and is known to us as 'Father,' when we recognize him within us as our Creator, as our mind, as our life, as our very being."

Unity's Statement of Faith, Articles 16 and 32 read as follows:

"We believe that creative Mind, God, is masculine and feminine, and that these attributes of Being are fundamental in both natural and spiritual man ... Almighty Father-Mother, we thank Thee for this vision of Thine Omnipotence, omniscience, and omnipresence, in us and in all that we think and do, in the name of Jesus Christ. Amen."

And who is this Jesus Christ?

On page 2 of **What Practical Christianity Stands For** we read:

"Statements for the Realization of the Son of God:

"I am the Son of God, and the Spirit of the Most High dwells in me."

"I am the only begotten Son, dwelling in the bosom of the Father."

"I am the Lord of my mentality and the ruler of all its Thought-People."

"I am the Christ of God."

"As the oak is in the acorn, so God is in man." Etc.

Unity literature notwithstanding, the unity of Unity is a unity with Christian Science and New Thought.

Unity suggests such daily thoughts as: "Prosperity follows prosperous thinking. For this reason I am thinking prosperous thoughts, wasting no time worrying about what I seem to lack." "I always think of substance as being abundant and sufficient for all needs. Therefore my material needs are always bountifully supplied."

Orison Swett Marden, whose books on New Thought were greedily read thirty-five years ago, wrote:

"When we feel a sense of unity, and at-oneness with the Creator, we cannot fear, we cannot want, because we are in the very midst of the supply, in the very lap of abundance. It is impossible for God's image and likeness in man to reflect failure or poverty. Man's divine image reflects prosperity, riches that are royal, divine abundance that never fails, plenty that can never grow less."

When these systems of thought warn against worry, fear, and advocate self-control versus the explosive passions, they are administering wholesome advice; but they render such advice vicious by adding that man must realize his divinity.

What then is the great sin of pantheism?

That it denies the cardinal doctrine of Scripture. The cardinal doctrine of Scripture is its teaching concerning God. And that doctrine is trinitarian.

In this the Bible stands apart from all other socalled sacred books. At the same time, here lies also the reason why only the Bible teaches salvation as the work of God.

For the Trinity of God means first of all the unity of God. God is **transcendent**, that is, distinct from and infinitely above his creation. The Sistine Madonna is not Raphael. Neither is God human, nor is man divine.

Every pantheist who denies that distinction ends in manworship. He knows nothing of salvation, for he knows no God to reach down from heaven to lift man out of misery. Mental power, which may temporarily avert or heal sickness, real or imaginary, cannot deliver from the power of death which is the wages of sin.

Fundamental to scriptural teaching is the unity and transcendence of God. **Hear, O Israel; Jehovah our God is one Jehovah: and thou shalt love Jehovah thy God with all thy heart, and with all thy soul, and with all thy might, Deut. 6:4, 5. I am the first, and I am the last; and besides me there is no God ... Is there a God besides me? Yea, there is no Rock; I know not any, Isa. 44:6, 8. The God that made**

—45—

the world and all things therein, he, being Lord of heaven and earth, dwelleth not in temples made with hands, Acts 17:24.

However, a mere doctrine of divine transcendence leads only to the fatalism of Mohammed, or the deism of the eighteenth and nineteenth centuries. A merely transcendent God is remote from man and meddles not in human affairs.

The scriptural doctrine includes that God dwells in man (divine immanence). It is **not** "the spirit of Jesus" (**spirit** with a small s, in which **spirit** becomes a synonym for **mood, temperament, mentality**), but God Himself, the third Person of the Holy Trinity, entering into man to renew and sanctify him. **Know ye not that ye are a temple of God, and that the Spirit of God dwelleth in you? I Cor. 3:16.**

And this immanence or indwelling of the sovereign God Who is above all has become possible to the sinner only because the Second Person of the divine Trinity (that is, Unity of Three), God the Son, has tabernacled among men, adding sinless human nature to his divine nature, that He might become—not a medium; **not** a man taken over by a "world-soul" or Principle; **not** a man more divine than others; but—the **Mediator,** at once God and man, that He might bridge the chasm left yawning by human rebellion beween God the Creator and man the creature, and thus restore in man God's image of an intelligent and moral human nature.

Unity, therefore, has no right to call itself a School of Christianity. It has no business adorning its pamphlets with the traditional likeness of Jesus Christ.

For it murders the Scriptures wherever it lays its pantheistic hands on them.

Thus in the Unity Sunday-School literature all of Scripture is spiritualized away and given a foreign meaning. Samaria becomes "the highest point of the intellectual perception of **Truth, or the department of objective consciousness that functions through the head."** Peter was a fisherman, and "a fisherman is symbolical of a consciousness that

—46—

is open to and seeking new ideas." "King Herod represents the ego in the outer or sense consciousness. The Herod man is temporal because he does not understand his origin or the law of his being. . . . Such a man does not fulfill the divine idea of a man, and another ego must supplant him. Jesus represents God's idea of a man in expression: Christ is that idea in the absolute . . . The wise-Men from the east are the inner planes of consciousness, which, like books of life, have kept the records of past lives and held them in reserve against the great day in which the soul should receive the supreme ego, Jesus."

In one other respect Unity has far outstripped Christian Science and other healing cults, namely, in the matter of advertising and organization. "The Unity School of Christianity," Kansas City, Missouri, regularly publishes six magazines **(Daily Word, Good Business, Progress, Unity, Weekly Unity and Wee Wisdom)**. It recommends, "Build yourself a Unity library," a recent catalogue listing titles of 28 "Unity Textbooks" and numerous smaller publications. It runs the "best equipped vegetarian restaurant in the world" as well as its own radio station. It has its own oil wells, well-ventilated and large class rooms and dormitories amidst beautiful surroundings. It sends thousands of healing and inspiring messages by mail, wire and telephone across the continent; its literature is read "in 88 foreign countries." In the words of C. W. Ferguson: Unity is "an enormous mail order concern dispensing health and happiness on the large scale of modern business enterprise . . . . It has transformed the U. S. mail into a missionary machine. It is the work of a retired realtor and his inspired wife, and with its tedious array of tabular facts and its insufferable efficiency, it suggests pretty well what Americans want in the realm of the spirit."

Well, yes, many of them.

But fortunately not all of them by any means!

VII

MORMONISM

EACH Sunday at nine o'clock in the morning from Temple Square, Salt Lake City, Utah. Alexander Schreiner is at the famous organ. J. Spencer Cornwall conducts the well-trained choir. The spoken word is by Richard Evans. The man has a mellow, persuasive voice. Moreover, he warns us that "it is not enough to be sincere, for one may be sincerely wrong, and therefore all the more wrong: we must not only be sincere, but sincerely right."

Of late Albert E. Bowen, "one of the quorum of twelve apostles," has added his voice on Sunday evenings. He warns against loss of our religion, antagonism against Christianity, and quotes from various Christian sources. No hobbies are ridden. It is just plain Christianity, without explanations, that is held aloft. And why not? Is not the name of the Church "The Church of Jesus Christ of Latter-Day Saints"?

So it came to pass that thousands of Americans, too much involved in making money to look into the tenets of anything of a metaphysical nature, have gradually adopted the view that the Utah movement stands for just one more type of Christianity. "Don't they use all the same hymns we sing? Isn't it an inspiration to listen to their broadcasts?

It surely is. But they do not tell you what they believe. If they did, America would throw up its hands in holy horror.

Or, is it true that to the younger generation Mormonism means just business and politics; that they have discarded its odious doctrines?

Perhaps some have. But the "Church" maintains the same organization with a President, Twelve Apostles, Aaronic and Melchizedec Priesthood and endless rigmarole; it has never repudiated any one of its heathen doctrines;

and practically all its young men still donate from one to two years going about as "missionaries" to all lands.

With this chapter we leave the field of pantheism. We have found the Isms we discussed in the last four chapters to be all pantheistic. Their sin is that they have exchanged the Christian heritage for the old paganism of the East. The Hindu Vivekananda told his Chicago audience in 1893: "Ye are divinities on earth. Sinners! It is a sin to call a man so. It is a standing libel on human nature." Should America return to that, surely America's doom would be sealed.

Jehovah's Witnesses, like Mormonism, is not pantheistic. They are rather anthropomorphic, that is, they conceive of God after the image of man. It does not follow, however, that they are therefore less vicious. Pantheism is not the only evil. And we cover our faces with shame when we pause to reflect that these two systems are of simon-pure American make.

Mormonism began with "Joseph Smith Jr. the Seer," who at the age of twenty-five organized "the Church of Jesus Christ of Latter-Day Saints" at Fayette, New York, in 1830. The utterly disreputable character of Smith, the hoax of the "golden plates," his lustful nature, his financial dishonesty—these and other things have been established so beyond all doubt that it is fruitless to waste our limited space in reviewing all that. If any one desires to know the truth of it all let him read the trilogy of Charles A. Shook: **Cumorah Revisited; The True Origin of Mormon Polygamy; The True Origin of the Book of Mormon.** He will find these books to be sufficient and incontrovertible.

We are, moveover, strongly inclined to believe that Brigham Young was absolutely sincere; that he firmly believed that Smith was a prophet. We are convinced that Mr. Young, though he had only eleven days of schooling, was a born leader and a statesman of no mean ability.

It is also fully conceded that the Mormons have proved excellent colonizers and have done much to develop the West. And during World War II their mutual aid organization has put the nation to shame.

We are also minded to omit for the present a discussion of the Mormon oath "to avenge the blood of Joseph the martyr and Hyrum his brother upon this nation;" and the statement of Bishop Lunt in 1880, "We will hold the balance of power and will dictate to the country." This pamphlet deals with false religions; in proportion as the false religion of Mormonism can be broken its political menace will vanish.

Many Americans think that when in 1896 "Zion" had "bowed to the Gentiles" in the matter of polygamy and Utah had been admitted to statehood, the innocent pastime of polygamy disappeared forever, and Mormonism settled down to a more orthodox Christianity. Nothing could be farther from the truth. Why do the thousands of mormon missionaries admit in re polygamy, when they are pressed, "We believe in it, but do not practice it"? They do not (?) practice it because they were compelled by threats of an invading U. S. Army to drop the matter. They believe in it because Mormon teachings are built upon it.

It makes no difference how Mormon polygamy originated. As to when and where it began there can be no doubt. It began with Joseph Smith who advocated plurality of wives very, very carefully in 1830 in the Book of Mormon, and in 1843 came out more boldly with a "Revelation on the Eternity of the Marriage Covenant" in his **Doctrine and Covenants**, which is officially considered to have been divinely inspired. But how it originated with Smith, whether from lust or from "principle," matters not. All the early Mormon leaders practiced polygamy, and the rejection of it by the Josephites or Reorganized Church of Jesus Christ of Latter-Day Saints, thriving in the eastern and midwest states, is just an illogical step that was taken under pressure of the "Gentiles."

Let us adopt the view of Brigham Young's daughter that her father's "strictly puritanical training ill-fitted him to accept such a doctrine ... that the men and women who entered into such a relationship in early days did so from purely religious motives. It was a high and sacred undertaking with them, involving much suffering and sacrifice on the part of both men and women." That only proves two things: that they were "sincerely wrong," to quote our Utah announcer of the plaintive voice; and that polygamy is of the very warp and woof of Mormonism.

How did it get to be that way?

Mormonism begins with a gross theory of polytheism (faith in many gods). There is not one God, but there are a great number of gods, all of whom were formerly men on the earth. When believers (Mormons) die, they also become gods. They will continue to have bodies of flesh and bones. They will also continue to propagate, for they will be male and female. They will populate the stars with their offspring.

Strange to say, the Bible is called in for support. For anything may be proven from the Bible, if one will only quote an isolated text and disregard its context. So when Jesus was asked by the Sadducees how there could be a resurrection, for one woman had outlived seven husbands, whose wife of the seven would she be in the resurrection? Jesus replied that they erred because they knew not the Scriptures, for in the resurrection they neither marry nor are given in marriage, but are as angels in heaven, **Matthew 22:30** Seeing that Scripture teaches that angels are spiritual beings without sex, that means, of course, that the woman won't be the wife of any of the seven, since there will be no sex, conseqently no marriage in heaven. But the Mormons say it means, No new marriages will be contracted in the resurrection life; therefore all marriages must be solemnized on earth, for this life only, or "sealed for eternity" in the secret temples of Mormonism. To remain single would mean that a woman can not reign in heaven as a queen by the side of a kingly husband; she could only occupy the role of a servant. It is therefore better to be a plural wife than no wife at all while in this life.

If, however, a woman is "sealed for eternity" to a man here on earth, that marriage will produce children through-

—51—

out eternity, for the stars must be populated. "O candidates for celestial glory!" exclaimed a "saint" of reputation, "Would your joys be full in the countless years of eternity without forming the connections, the relationship, the kindred ties which concentrate in the domestic circle, branch forth, and bud and blossom, and bear fruits of eternal increase? Would that eternal emotion of charity and benevolence which swells your bosoms be satisfied to enjoy in 'single blessedness' without an increase in posterity, those exhaustless stores of never ending riches and enjoyments? Or, would you, like your heavenly Father, prompted by eternal benevolence and charity, wish to fill countless millions of worlds with your begotten sons and daughters and to bring them through all the gradations of progressive being, to inherit immortal bodies and eternal mansions in your several dominions?"

Hard to believe? Read it yourself in Parley Pratt's **Key to the Science of Theology,** page 151 (7th edition, Salt Lake City. Deseret News. 1925).

Nor is this all.

A woman should also be "sealed for time." The gods, formerly men on earth, are even now begetting children as spirits; these spirit-children are waiting in heaven to receive bodies on earth. Hence it is the duty of every man and woman to produce as many infant human bodies as possible. The heathen doctrines of the pre-existence of souls and of polygamy (better a polygamous wife than none at all!) are interwoven in Mormonism.

Does any one think that just because Mormonism lies low through "Gentile" pressure, the system has changed? That no "sealing for eternity" takes place in the secret rites in the inaccessible temples in Salt Lake City, Mesa, Arizona, and soon in Los Angeles and Idaho Falls?

Shall we just pronounce this heathenism innocent? Or opine that the rest of its theology is Christian? The many gods are "big men, like Brigham Young." So the doctrine of the Trinity was murdered as follows:

"The Father has a body of flesh and bones as tangible as man's; the Son also: but the Holy Ghost has not a body of flesh and bones but is a personage of spirit . . . Were it not so, the Holy Ghost could not dwell in us. A man may receive the Holy Ghost, and it may descend upon him and not tarry with him"—Joseph Smith in **Doctrine and Covenants.**

What can be left of our Lord in such a "theology"?

"When the Virgin Mary conceived the child Jesus, the Father had begotten him in his own likeness. He was NOT begotten by the Holy Ghost. And who was the Father? He was the first of the human family . . . Jesus, our elder brother, was begotten in the flesh by the same character that was in the garden of Eden, and who is our Father in heaven—" Brigham Young, **Journal of Discourses, 1:50.**

"When our father Adam came into the garden of Eden, he came into it with a celestial body, and brought Eve, one of his wives, with him . . . He is our Father and our God, and the only God with whom we have to do—Brigham Young, **Ibidem.**

"Jesus Christ was a polygamist; Mary and Martha, the sisters of Lazarus, were his plural wives, and Mary Magdalene was another. Also, the bridal feast of Cana of Galilee, ... was on the occasion of one of his own marriages" —Brigham Young.

Literally every Bible doctrine is denied or twisted into its opposite by the "Saints." Of the biblical doctrine of justification Talmadge wrote, "The sectarian dogma of justification by faith alone has exercised an influence for evil since the early days of Christianity." Instead of Romans 1-5 and Galatians 1-3 the Mormons teach as follows:

Adam found himself in a position that impelled him to disobey either one of two divine laws: the law to multiply, or that other law to abstain from eating the forbidden fruit. Had he obeyed the latter command, he could not have been united with Eve, who was in the state of sin. Therefore he "deliberately and wisely" chose the lesser sin, ate of the fruit and fulfilled the greater commandment to replenish the earth. "Adam fell that men might be."

Jesus Christ made atonement for this minor sin, and "by his expiatory sacrifice made it possible for man to be redeemed, restored, resurrected and exalted to the elevated position designed for him in the creation as a Son of God." But Christ only redeemed men ("all peoples, nations and tongues") from temporal death. From spiritual death man redeems himself "through obedience to His law"—John Taylor, **The Mediation and Atonement.**

Even this brief discussion of Mormonism would not be complete without a few references to the fraud known as **The Book of Mormon.** "The Church of Christ," headquarters on the Temple Lot, Independence, Missouri, publishers of **Zion's Advocate,** a monthly journal, deny that they are Mormons or Latter-Day Saints. They disown every publication of the Utah or the Iowa (Brighamite and Josephite) Mormons. They deny that Joseph Smith was inspired when he published **The Holy Scriptures. Translated and Corrected by the Spirit of Revelation,** by Joseph Smith Jr., the Seer; but affirm that he was divinely inspired when he translated the "Golden Plates" with the "Urim and Thummin" given him by the angel Moroni on the hill Cumorah, and the Book of Mormon was the inspired result.

But the book of Mormon taken by itself is sufficient to mark the entire ungodly business as a huge fraud.

The **Book of Mormon** tells the story of two entirely different early American peoples, Jaredites who came from the tower of Babel under Jared and his brother, crossing the Atlantic Ocean in 344 days in eight "cigar-shaped barges" (written A. D. 420!), and located in Central America. They came to an end after some 1600 years, about 600 B. C. as a result of dissensions and revolts. The second history describes the adventures of Lehi's four sons, Laman, Lemuel, Sam and Nephi, which Nephi left Jerusalem in the time of Zedekiah, and arrived "on the coast of Chile, not far from the thirtieth degree, south latitude." Nephi at once began to record the history of his people upon metal plates. His descendant Moroni, a prince of royal blood, finished the plates and hid them in the hill Cumorah in New York, A. D. 420. There they were revealed to the prophet Joseph Smith Jr. in 1823. Consider the following:

1. The Book of Mormon boldly asserts that the word of God and the knowledge of truth were lost from the earth from 420 to 1823. Yet the book contains more than 1000 citations from the Bible, and these are all given in the King James version of 1611!

2. The entire history as contained in the Book of Mormon is a hoax which contradicts all that has been discovered and unearthed concerning early aborigenes in the Americas. For details read **The Mormons and Their Bible** by M. T. Lamb. Judson Press.

3. The Book of Mormon tells of so-called miracles, which are cheap stunts and a reflection upon all that is known of God. Imagine God causing "a skin of blackness" to come upon an entire people because they are too beautiful and might become a temptation to God's people; and 500 years later, presto! removing the skin of blackness, and hence we have both Black Indians and White Indians in America. Fancy God touching stones with his finger in order to make them illumine the cigar-shaped barges in which the windows have been forgotten! Etc., etc.

4. Joseph Smith translated the Book of Mormon under divine inspiration, from the Golden Plates; yet the book contains such grammatical niceties as: "Yea, if my days had been in them days ... But behold, I am consigned that these are my days." "And they, having been waxed strong in battle, that they might not be destroyed." "Even until they had arriven at the land of Middoni." And so forth!

Let us hope that the American public will bear in mind some of these things while listening to the spoken word by Richard Evans!

VIII

BRITISH-ISRAELISM

SURELY, the devil has all kinds of baits for all kinds of people. He also fosters silly delusions which may be harbored by believers and unbelievers alike. A minister enters a ministerial association meeting armed with a heavy tome, proceeds to lecture on the Great Pyramid of Egypt, and concludes with the statement, "Brethren, I was a modernist until I discovered this great truth; I owe my return to the evangelical faith to my discovery of the British-Israel theory; I now know that the word of God does not remain unfulfilled." But another man may proceed from the same pyramid, and find his reading of these measurements and their mystical interpretation incorrect, and abandon faith in Scripture. We remember how "Pastor" Russell bolstered his theory of Christ's return in 1874 upon this same pyramid (afterward condemned by Rutherford).

The B.-I. Theory, also parading as Anglo-Israelism, Celto-Saxon, Destiny of America, The Lost Ten Tribes, has this in common with Mormonism that it teaches that the "Lost Tribes" are now living in America. The Mormons trace them via Nephites and Lamanites to Central America to which their ancestors came at the time of Zedekiah; the B. I. trace them to America via Great Britain from the days of the same Zedekiah. Mormons see the fulfillment of the O. T. prophecy in the discovery of "white Indians" in Mexico awaiting the arrival of a "white brother" to lead them to Missouri;[1] Anglo Israelites find the fulfillment of the same prophecies in the leading position which Britain, America and Australia occupy in the economic and interna-

---

1. Cf. *The Chaos of Cults*, 1951 ed.

tional world. "The Anglo-saxon race is the literal and blood descendant of the ten tribes of Israel whom Shalmaneser deported into Media in the eighth century B. C. and who hitherto have been completely lost."

They base this assertion upon a so-called exegesis which follows "the pattern of history." That is to say, promises made to Israel, regardless of whether they were meant spiritually or materially, and were conditional or unconditional, are taken in a grossly literal and material sense; they are then referred to nations living today; and a search is made for the nations to which these literally understood promises may apply. The latter is done in a facile manner and with a latitude of interpretation. For instance:

When Jacob predicted that Joseph was to become a **fruitful bough; his branches run over the wall**, Gen. 49:22; and in Isa. 49:20 we read that after the captivity the people will say, **The place is too strait for me; give place to me that I may dwell**, it is evident that we must look for a nation that has departed from England where the anglo-saxon sons of Israel dwell. Then, if we add to this that Jacob said of Manasseh, **His seed shall become a multitude of nations**, Gen. 49:19, we have at once that "overwhelming evidence" to which the B. I. are fond to refer: Great Britain is Ephraim, and that meltingpot of many nations, the U. S. A. is Manasseh—and that stands even if the wall became an ocean and the Ephraimites became sons of Manasseh merely by going over that watery "wall."

And there is much more evidence. **Thou shalt lend unto many nations, and thou shalt not borrow,** was spoken to Israel, Deut. 28:12. "This prophecy is fulfilled by no other nation but Great Britain. Every other nation has borrowed, and that from Great Britain, but she has borrowed from none. Great Britain receives yearly 50 or 60 millions of pounds sterling in interest upon her loans to other nations (written in 1941). Let us be glad that some of Britain's sons have gone "over the wall"; that leaves room for postwar Lend Lease from Uncle Sam.

Again: sabbath observance was to be **a sign between me and you throughout your generations, Ex. 31:13**—and have not Britain and the U. S. A. alone had "blue laws" **as over** against the "continental sabbath"? Even Voltaire said, "Whether Englishmen know it or not, it is the English Sunday which makes England what it is." And Dr. Ryle, late bishop of Liverpool, wrote, "I assert without hesitation that the only countries on the face of the globe in which you will find a true observance of the sabbath are Great Britain and her colonies."

Such is the scheme; and this is the method. Of course, having once distilled all this from Scripture by quoting and applying texts following the mere sound of words, B. I. also have to substantiate their theory with arguments obtained from history. Rather—for history is of comparatively recent origin—they borrow freely from tradition, for: "Tradition is the basis of all earlier history." Whatever tradition fits into the "pattern" seems to be appreciated.

It is established by the roundabout path of tradition that Jeremiah took with him out of Egypt a daughter of Zedekiah, and also the "stone of destiny" upon which Jacob had **rested his head at Bethel when he fled into Haran. The** king's daughter (altho Zedekiah was king only by appointment **of Nebuchadnezzar and not according to divine ar**rangement), married an Irish chieftain or king; and the stone of destiny became the stone of scone upon which the English kings have been crowned via the Scottish and Irish kings in earlier years—and so the evidence is amply both in the flesh and in stone that the kings of Britain are the true house of David.

But "how come" that the house of David should rule in London? This is because Israel traveled via the Crimea, the Black Sea, the Danube river into Scandinavia and western Europe, captured England from the Britons, and divided the country into sections which all remind us of God's promise, **In Isaac shall thy seed be called, Gen. 21:12.**: Sussex, or South Saxon, **Essex**, or East Saxon; **Middlesex**, etc. And why Saxon? Because Saxon really means Saac's sons, Isaac's sons.

You won't believe it? Then hear the rest of it: **British** stands for **berith-ish, berith** being Hebrew for **covenant,** and **ish** for man; i.e. men of the covenant; and **John Bull** was so named because Isaac's sons in Britain naturally frequently sacrificed a **bullock,** which in Hebrew spells **engle, hence England.**

And, by the way, **Samurai,** the name of the ancient Japanese military caste, sounds much like **Samaria,** capital of Israel; hence the Japanese also must be traced to Israel. No wonder we Israelites have of late been talking of taking these erstwhile enemies into a covenant with us against the communists!

There are many other evidences that the Anglo-saxons are indeed Isaac's sons, and these are found in similarities between ancient and modern tombstones, crosses and circles; but unfortunately all scientific encyclopedias reject all these inferences, the Britannica leading with words such as these: "utterly unsound," "historically and anthropologically unsound."

It is easy not only to quote poetry from Sir Walter Scott in support of the Stone of Scone legend, and to write, "It is a dull reddish sandstone; there is none other like it in Britain. Geologists tell us that it belongs to a sandstone formation near the Dead Sea"; and to add the mysterious information that though this stone has been resting in Westminster Abbey since 1298 A. D. and before that lay in the church of Iona where Fergus the Great was crowned upon it in A. D. 498, yet "Its rings are worn by years of carrying" (by the Israelites thru the wilderness journey, and presumably the united effort of old man Jeremiah and the blooming young daughter of Zedekiah). But it is rather disconcerting that in the face of all such scientific tradition Dr. A. C. Ramsey of the Department of Geology in London University after a thoro study of the stone both microscopically and chem-

—59—

ically, reported in 1865 that the stone of Destiny is a "calcareous sandstone of scottish origin."[1]

The harm and danger of the B. I. theory lies in the following facts:

1. It causes divisions between Christians and their fellows, B. I.'s meet in separate groups ignoring the churches to which they belong.

2. It makes a laughing stock of the Bible in the sight of skeptics when they are told that "orthodox" Christians resort to such methods of exegesis.

3. It causes men to trust in an arm of flesh; like the Pharisees of old, English and Americans, South Africans and Australians are told that they are God's chosen people, either by direct descent or by adoption into Israel.

4. It shifts the emphasis upon God's promises from the spiritual to the material and economic, from the everlasting to the transient, and would lull us to sleep in a time of world distress, substituting for the one-time Pax Romanica and Hitler's dream of a Pax Germanica a fancied Pax Saxonica.

5. It makes a stench in the nostrils of communists and other foes of the democratic nations by declaring them to be invincible according to Isaiah 54:17, and stating that their foot shall be upon the neck of their enemies.

It will be clear that all such fanciful theories as to early American history as animate Mormons and British-Israelites stand or fall with this one basic dogma: Ever since the Ten Tribes had been carried away in 721 B. C. and the Two Tribes in 585 B. C., the names Israel and Judah denote two separate peoples. "The Bible is perfectly plain. When it speaks of Israel, in ninety-nine cases out of a hundred the ten tribes are meant."

---

1. Fred Haberman, *Tracing Our Ancestors*. Kingdom Press, St. Petersburg, Fla., 1934, p. 159. W. H. Smith, *The Ten Tribes of Israel Never Lost*. Vancouver, B. C., 1946, p. 117. The latter is one of the most eminent, concise and scholarly works against the entire theory.

If, therefore, this is against the clear facts of Scripture the entire theory of Destiny of America tumbles down. The facts are as follows:

Isaiah (8th century B. C.) said that Judah and Israel would be persecuted together but find that they had one Redeemer, 50:33. They were to return together, 11:12.

Jeremiah (7th century): Israel and Judah would return to Palestine together, 3:18.

Hosea said the same thing, 1:11.

Ezra sacrificed twelve bullocks according to the number of tribes that had returned, 6:17, and called them "all Israel," 2:70. Of course, they were a minority, but that holds of the Two Tribes as well as of the Ten; the point is that these are called God's people, Israel, Judah. The others were amalgamated among the nations.

"The word Israel is used 83 times, and the word Judah is used 174 times as names of the united people. The extent of Jewry is seen in Acts 2:5."

Paul was an Israelite, a Jew, and a Hebrew, all in one. Paul said that in his day the twelve tribes of Israel looked earnestly for the hope of Israel. Jesus had sent his disciples to the lost sheep of the house of Israel.

For that matter, even before the division in the days of Rehoboam, the names Israel and Judah are used alternatively for both groups together (see **Ex.** 16:31; 4:38; **Lev.** 10:6, etc., fourteen times in all; and compare with **II Sam.** 2:4, 7; 12:8; **I Chron.** 28:4. Also mark the expression "princes of Judah" as used, after the division, of Israel, **II Chron.** 22:8). But why quote more?

The evidence is abundant; the verdict is inevitable.

IX

THE CHRISTIAN RELIGION

IS THERE, then, no objective source of information concerning God and His relation to us? Is there nowhere an authoritative statement? Amidst an ever growing number of false cults, and a vast number of disagreeing Christian denominations, is it impossible to state what is the real Christian religion?

Surely, there are too many denominations in the United States of America. In our thinly populated State of Washington I came upon a town of 2400 in which 28 churches are represented. People mockingly call it "the holy City."

Individualism. Inability to co-operate. Refusal to see eye-to-eye. These pronounced American weaknesses, rather than firm conviction, have, in all too many cases, given rise to disruption and schism.

Some day, perhaps, God will cleanse us by means of persecution from the filth of our disobedience to Christ's will that Christians should be one **that the world may believe that thou didst send me, John 17:21.** For if there are no atheists in foxholes, there can be little display of denominationalism in concentration camps.

A candid appraisal of facts, however, will lead to the frank admission that the church's divided existence is not the sole reason why entire towns lie asleep when on Sunday mornings a few straggly worshipers answer the call to prayer. There are things that are worse than either radical or minor difference of opinion in matters religious. Among these is a total indifference to all religious conviction.

Moreover, if those who sneer at the Church would take the trouble to examine the credentials of the various Christian churches, they might discover a remarkable unity and agreement on fundamentals far beyond their expectation.

Our troubles lie far deeper. The great heritage of the Christian church, so painstakingly arrived at, so profoundly thought through and so zealously guarded again and again at the cost of blood and tears, has been brushed aside by multitudes who have come to the loose belief that a varnish of outward morality will do as a substitute for Christianity. We have come to the point where a none too pessimistic religious weekly has stated editorially: "An honest appraisal requires the ackowledgment that American Protestantism is spiritually weaker today than at any time in its history. [1] And again: "It is no exaggeration to say that, since the time when the invention of printing gave the Bible to the common people . . . there has been no generation of Christians so religiously illiterate as our own." [2]

There are those among us who are convinced that the Christian religion has been God's greatest boon to mankind; that it has removed barbarism and illiteracy; that it has promoted the more abundant life of art and science, of high moral standards to be found nowhere outside the pale of Christendom.

They hold that when these byproducts of Christianity are relished while their fountainhead is trodden under foot, God calls the Christianized nations back by turning their boasted civilization against them lest a worse evil befall them.

Such a time is upon us even now.

Are we heeding the divine voice that calls us back to the Father? Or are we seeking oblivion in alcohol and fornication, in wholesale denunciation of other nations as evil and indiscriminate praise of our own American goodness?

It should not be an impossible task to determine what is the essence of the Christian religion.

---

1. Chas. C. Morrison, "Protestant Reorientation" in *The Christian Century*, October 27, 1943.

2. The same in *Christian Century*, Dec. 1, 1943.

If God is infinite and man finite, man can but know God because He has made Himself known.

It is equally sure, when God wants to be known, He can reveal Himself in such a manner that man may respond to His self-revelation. And His unveiling of Himself must needs be consistent throughout: there may have been progress but there can be no contradiction.

Ever since its beginning Christendom has believed that God has spoken to man in the Bible and, at the same time, that the Holy Spirit must guide the human mind that it may both understand the divine revelation in Scripture and love it.

For man is not only finite; he is also depraved. Sin has affected all men, at all times and in all places, so as to make them inclined to follow error in stead of truth, to drift toward evil rather than to excel in goodness.

Above all, man is so sinful that he puts his own interests far ahead of God's honor and the promotion of His cause on earth: many men and women will dismiss the suggestion that they are sinful with the reply that they "have never done anything out of the way," and they fail to realize that their great sin is that "God is not in all their thoughts."

All have sinned, and fall short of the glory of God, is the fundamental biblical statement concerning man. This is written in **Romans 3:23,** but the same thought runs through all the Scriptures. **For we are all become as one that is unclean,** said the greatest of the Old Testament prophets, **and all our righteousnesses are as a polluted garment: and we all do fade as a leaf; and our iniquities, like the wind, take us away, Isaiah 64:4.** You are, said Jesus to those Jews who gloried in being Abraham's seed, **of your father the devil, and the lusts of your father it is your will to do, John 8:44.** Neither did Jesus distinguish between bad men and good men as though the latter were to be congratulated because there was so little of imperfection left in them; but, **Every**

one that committeth sin is the bondservant of sin, John 8:34.

Isaiah's statement that our iniquities, like the wind, carry us away is but the poetic phrasing of the common scriptural teaching that **the wages of sin is death, Rom. 6:23; that God cannot be tempted with evil, and he himself tempteth no man: but each man is tempted when he is drawn away by his own lust and enticed. Then the lust, when it hath conceived, beareth sin: and the sin, when it is full grown, bringeth forth death, James 1:13-15.**

According to Scripture neither sin nor death can possibly be the result of evolution; they are the fruits of a fall. Sin, therefore, is not a disaster, or a weakness to which man is heir as a result of his brute ancestry; quite to the contrary, it is the effect of willful, uncalled for rebellion against a good God who had created man able to know the will of his Creator and to recognize it as only good, wise and beneficial.

Thus the Christian religion, the only religion which offers a gospel worthy of the name, begins with condemning man and holding him solely responsible for the evil condition that has him in its iron grip. The Bible is not like a charlatan who puts some salve on a sore spot and calls it whole while underneath a deadly gangrene does its vicious work. It is rather like a surgeon who cuts deeply, but his cutting is an act of kindness because he removes the source of evil.

The very first requisite, therefore, in order to get rid of evil in its every form is the humble acknowledgment of one's lost condition. **Only acknowledge thine iniquity, that thou hast transgressed against Jehovah thy God, Jeremiah 3:13.** Salvation begins with David's confession, **Against thee, thee only, have I sinned, and done that which is evil in thy sight; that thou mayest be justified when thou speakest, and be clear when thou judgest, Psalm 51:4.**

When man has arrived at the point where he blames neither God nor his fellow, ill luck nor circumstances, but only himself for his transgressions, he is ready to benefit by the gospel. **For the sacrifices of God are a broken spirit: a broken and a contrite heart, O God, thou wilt not despise, Psalm 51:17.**

For only the gospel, in contrast with every so-called "great religion" and every false cult, begins with casting man down in his pride and continues with holding before him the unfathomed, infinite love of God, Who being offended, mended the breach in His own Person and at infinite cost.

It has become quite fashionable to refer to the devil, that archenemy of mankind, as to a mythical boomerang, and to speak of hell as a fictitious place to which we lightheartedly consign our enemies.

Back of this lies the hatred of the natural, that is, the sinful heart against divine truth. Ignoring the righteousness of God which cannot tolerate evil, this spirit steps lightly (Christian Science, Modernism) or roughly (Russellism) over Jesus' words, **There shall be the weeping and the gnashing of teeth, Matt. 8:12.** For it ignores or minimizes the O. T. verdict, so clearly corroborated by the world in which we live today: **The heart is deceitful above all things, and it is exceedingly corrupt: who can know it? I, Jehovah search the mind, I try the heart, even to give every man according to his ways, according to the fruit of his doings, Jeremiah 17:9.** And the N. T. words, **It is appointed unto men once to die, and after this cometh judgment, Heb. 9:27.**

Since this cardinal truth has been tampered with and toned down, Christianity has been gradually diluted to a **wishy-washy help-yourself-religiousness,** in which Jesus Christ has become the pattern of clean living, just a few steps ahead of the rest of us in moral evolution.

The denial of the deadly character of sin is serious not only because it belittles God's holiness and righteousness; it also detracts from the love of God. Had sin been less enormous, God might have paid a smaller price for the redemption of mankind; but now it was only in the cross of Christ that "righteousness and peace have kissed each other." The love of God, concerning which we thoughtlessly quote the most famous Bible verse **(John 3:16), is so incomparably great**: First, because it was for sinners that God gave His Son though God is too pure to have a share in iniquity and can experience only revulsion against sin; **secondly**, because with His Only begotten Son God gave His divine all to the point of entering into the sinful human race; and **thirdly** because God "gave up" the Son **who is in the bosom of the Father, John 1:18, to the point where He was made sin on our behalf, II Cor. 5:21, having become a curse for us, Gal. 3:13.**

Refusal to accept this gift of infinite love therefore constitutes the greatest sin, whether it be done in blasphemous insolence or in politely passing by the supreme sacrifice. **Is it nothing to you, all ye that pass by? Behold, and see if there be any sorrow like unto my sorrow which is brought upon me, Wherewith Jehovah hath afflicted me in the day of his fierce anger, Lament. 1:12. All we like sheep have gone astray; we have turned every one to his own way; and Jehovah hath laid on him the iniquity of us all, Isa. 53:6.**

But our Bible is nothing if it is not consistent. God forsooth does not teach that **out of the heart come forth evil thoughts, murders, adulteries, fornications, thefts, false witnesses, railings, Matt. 15:19,** only to state in the same breath that man may at any time change his Ethiopian's **skin or his leopard's spots and "accept Jesus," as a good** proposition which he considers it his worth while to look into. Man must be **born anew, born of the Holy Spirit,** says the Saviour, John 3:3, 5.

Being born again, however, is as much a thing to undergo as is being born of a woman: the beginning of salvation is of God and of Him alone.

> *I sought the Lord, and afterward I knew*
> *He moved my soul to seek Him, seeking me;*
> *It was not I that found, O Saviour true;*
> *No, I was found of Thee.*

Thus the Bible deals with the sinner in true pedagogical style: Having laid the responsibility at man's door, it guards against indifference and false passivity; then, having reminded man that he cannot even begin to save himself, it casts him back upon the Lord as the sole author of his salvation.

This done, the Scriptures give the penitent sinner full encouragement in the words of Jesus: **No man can come to me, except the Father that sent me draw him; and, CONSEQUENTLY: and him that cometh to me I will in no wise cast out. John 6:37, 44.** For the Father and the Son cannot but work together.

Let, therefore, he who has seen his sin and dreaded its result, rejoice: Jesus Christ is able to save to the uttermost **them that draw near unto God through him, Heb. 7:25.** God is more willing than man is, **not wishing that any should perish, but that all should come to repentance, II Peter 3:9.** The thirst for salvation at His once pierced hands is itself unmistakable evidence of the saving process of the Father, by means of the Son, and applied by the Holy Spirit . . . **And he that is athirst, let him come: he that will, let him take the water of life freely,** is the Bible's final word, **Rev. 22:17.**

There is another point at which full salvation halts in the case of many who call themselves Christians, yet fail to let their light shine before men.

The word of God does not teach that **the Son of man came to give his life a ransom for many, Matt. 20:28,** only to stop there.

God removes sin as well as its consequence. **If we confess our sins, he is faithful and righteous to forgive us our sins, and to cleanse us from all unrighteousness, I John 1:9 and the blood of Jesus his Son cleanseth us from all sin, 1:7.**

Today the world is in a worse plight than it has ever been, not because Christianity has failed, but because it has never been seriously put to the test.

For where Christ holds undisputed sway He comes with His law of love, which love is the only thing that can destroy hatred; and hate has bred all the world's woe.

Then the Golden Rule is put into practice as well as admired; to do unto men as we would have them do unto us because God requires it results in true altruism, an altruism of individual toward fellow man, of class to class, between race and race, from nation to nation. Had their been a more universal and earnest endeavor to love God with all the heart and had we loved our neighbor as we should love ourselves —in other words, had there been more true Christianity— wars would have been abolished long ago, class hatred have been a thing of the past, racial antagonism would have disappeared; the Christian nations, rather than exploit the backward races, would have raised them to their own level of abundance for all; the "four freedoms" would have been an accomplished fact after more than nineteen centuries of the Christian religion, religious intolerance between Christians would be an unknown quantity.

The Scriptures, however, do not promise a gradual and total Christianization of the world in this age. To the contrary, they warn us that unbelief, selfishness and greed will wax worse. **But know this, that in the last days grievous times shall come. For men shall be lovers of self, lovers of money, boastful, haughty, railers, disobedient to parents, unthankful, unholy, without natural affection, implacable, slanderers, without self-control, fierce, no lovers of good, traitors, headstrong, puffed up, lovers of pleasure rather than lovers of God; holding a form of godliness, but having denied the power thereof; from these also turn away, II Timothy 3:1-5:** the reason why this booklet has been written.

But they do promise the visible return of the Son of man in great power and majesty, to judge the living and the dead. Then shall all wrongs be righted. Then shall the righteous shine as the firmament. A new heaven and a new earth will appear out of the conflagration of this old, sinstricken universe **(II Peter 3:10).** Then will the Son of man own His disciples, in spite of all their imperfection, and they shall enter with Him into the glory of eternal life **(Matt. 10:32; 25:46; I John 3:2).** Wars shall be no more **(Isa. 2:4),** nor tears **(Rev. 21:4)** ... **And there shall be no curse any more, Rev. 22:3. For Christ, having been once offered to bear the sins of many, shall appear a second time, apart from sin, to them that wait for him, unto salvation, Heb. 9:28.**

Thus our Lord Jesus Christ, Son of God and born of a woman, once slain, now exalted above all, is the center of the Christian religion. It is He that leads us to the Father **(John 1:12).** It is He that is the Christian's object of loyal service and adoration. And He is **Christ Jesus our hope, I Timothy 1:1.**

Like St. Paul, every Christian is a bondservant, that is, a slave, of Christ. But this bondage is true freedom: **If therefore the Son shall make you free, ye shall be free indeed, John 8:36.** For He delivers us from the bondage of Satan, and restores us **into the liberty of the glory of the children of God, Rom. 8:21.** This is the true freedom from want and freedom from fear. No evil can touch the Father's children, beloved in Christ. He may chasten, but will never punish them. He cares for them to the point of having numbered their very hairs **(Matt. 10:30),** and whatever seems to be to their hurt, He makes to work together to their ultimate gain **(Rom. 8:28).**

Harassing times are upon us. The present unrest is beyond human ken, and its dire aftermath may well prove past all previous human experience. Today's problems are staggering, and they raise questions of such gigantic proportions that it will call for the accumulated wisdom of the best heads in all lands to bring order out of chaos.

Yet there is one question that is of paramount importance.

More weighty it is than questions of post-war reconstruction.

More pertinent is this question than all the world's quest after peace, goodwill and mundane happiness.

It is the question that must be answered by every soul in the privacy of the inner chamber.

That question was answered wrongly by him who first asked it; answered wrongly for political reasons; answered wrongly to his everlasting sorrow.

It is the question of the Roman procurator Pontius Pilate.

That question must now be faced by every one who has read through these pages:

What shall I do then with Jesus which is called Christ? Matthew 27:22.